D1566370

THE RETURN OF
CHRISTIAN
HUMANISM

Out of What Chaos: A Novel (2007)

The Ethics of Modernism: Moral Ideas in Yeats, Eliot, Joyce, Woolf, and Beckett (2007)

T. S. Eliot and American Poetry (1998)

THE RETURN OF
CHRISTIAN
HUMANISM

CHESTERTON, ELIOT, TOLKIEN,
and the ROMANCE OF HISTORY

Lee Oser

University of Missouri Press
Columbia and London

PR
149
.H86
O84
2007

Library of Congress Cataloging-in-Publication Data

Oser, Lee, 1958-
    The return of Christian humanism : Chesterton, Eliot, Tolkien, and the romance of history /
Lee Oser.
        p.   cm.
    Summary: "Oser examines the twentieth-century literary clash between a dogmatically
relativist modernism and a robust revival of Christian humanism. Reviewing English literature
from Chaucer to Beckett, and the thoughts of philosophers, theologians, and modern literary
critics, Oser challenges the assumption that Christian orthodoxy is incompatible with
humanism, freedom, and democracy"—Provided by publisher.
    Includes bibliographical references and index.
    ISBN 978-0-8262-1775-2 (alk. paper)
    1. Humanism in literature. 2. English literature—History and criticism. 3. Christian
literature, English—History and criticism. 4. Theology, Doctrinal, in literature.
5. Christianity and literature—Great Britain—History. 6. Chesterton, G. K. (Gilbert Keith),
1874-1936—Criticism and interpretation. 7. Eliot, T. S. (Thomas Stearns), 1888-1965—
Criticism and interpretation. 8. Tolkien, J. R. R. (John Ronald Reuel), 1892-1973—Criticism
and interpretation. I. Title.
    PR149.H86O84 2007
    820.9'3823—dc22

                                                                                2007026461

Designer: Stephanie Foley
Typesetter: BookComp, Inc.
Printer and binder: Thomson-Shore, Inc.
Typefaces: Garamond Three and Goudy

    Acknowledgment is made as follows for permission to quote from copyrighted material:
Passages from "This Room," from *Your Name Here* by John Ashbery, copyright © 2000 by John
Ashbery, reprinted by permission of Georges Borchardt, Inc., on behalf of the author; United
Kingdom and Commonwealth rights granted by permission of Carcanet Press Limited.

FOR KATE, ELEANOR, AND BRIANA

Contents

PREFACE

At the heart of twentieth-century letters was the clash between a dogmatically relativist type of modernism and Christian humanism. This conflict, a crux in the western literary tradition, is still with us. It haunts our culture because relativism's most formidable opponent, in the marketplace of ideas, is a religious orthodoxy that salvages reason and nature. Not so much understood by its critics as travestied and dismissed, this orthodoxy has come to define, negatively, a postmodern academy that has forgotten the beauty in life.

It should not be a ticket to scholarly oblivion to suggest that all hinges, in the end, on spoken and unspoken religious beliefs. The subtle dependence not just of literature but of all culture on religion was a theme that rallied nineteenth-century romantic and neoromantic thinkers throughout Europe. Inspired by gothic architecture, François René de Chateaubriand defended the sacred in nature and history from the worst excesses of the Enlightenment. Coleridge, pursuing the creative imagination to its sources deep in the mind, returned to Genesis and the biblical God. In his magisterial essay "Christian Humanism through the Ages," Roman Catholic thinker Virgil Nemoianu recalls the rare and forgotten names of a great movement: Alois Gugler, Jaime Balmès, Donoso Cortés, Cardinal St. Clement Mary Hofbauer, the Oxford Tractarians (whose fame is rescued by Newman), Hannah More, and others. The list is poignantly long, of Christian visionaries who saw their religion giving birth to culture and art.

But who reads Chateaubriand today? A leading biography of Coleridge deals with his Christianity in an occasional passing reference. No one has even noticed that the Beatles were culturally Catholic, or that John Lennon was raised a Catholic Christian. Without scruple or debate, our schools condone the blindest intellectual prejudice of the twentieth century, and maybe the key to its horrors, the idea that religion is the enemy of art and culture. Conrad, Hardy, and Henry James did not think so. Bernard Shaw did, but his clever and well-crafted plays are too thin to last, too lacking in permanent human emotion. Like that other prophet of cruel frontiers, H. G. Wells, he supplied ideas to intellectual speculators who wanted to think big about the future and shed their moral anxieties along the way. By comparison, Woolf, Joyce, and Beckett were not propagandists: they were artists. They were aesthetes, but they were also spiritual writers obsessed with the soul. It was not the modernists themselves, but a cadre of specialists, usurping cultural authority, that ruled out the dialectic between religion and literature. The only good thing to be said for this situation is that it cannot last forever.

From their place in the recent past, Chesterton, Eliot, and Tolkien give us the chance for renewal and renaissance. Unlike their forebears in the nineteenth century, they wrote when the institutional arrangements of our own time were visible. In this sense, they had to start over. They were embattled but not wholly isolated figures, major writers in English who understood their art as an effort to keep the sacred wellsprings of culture open. The waters have gone underground, but like the mythical stream Arethusa they will come pouring into the light of day, if we know where to find them.

L. O.
March 25, 2007
Worcester, Massachusetts

ACKNOWLEDGMENTS

I am especially grateful to Virgil Nemoianu for his saving criticism. Over the years, Benjamin Lockerd has supplied Olympian doses of inspiration and help. I cannot thank him enough. Jeffrey Bloechl (*animae dimidium meae*) supplied expert guidance. My wife, Kathleen Lieuallen Oser, has nourished my ideas and made my writing possible. Thinking of friends, colleagues, teachers, and students, I also want to thank Catherine Corneille, Michelin Lockerd, Martin Lockerd, James Kee, Robert Cording, Joseph Lawrence, Marie Borroff, Maria Sciannameo, Robert Garvey, Christopher Ricks, Jeffrey Shoulson, Blaise Nagy, Donald Brand, David Schaefer (*l'homme de bon courage*), David and Amanda Bonagura, Richard Matlak, Jonathan Mulrooney, Victoria Rosenberg (who introduced a young boy to the wonders of Tolkien), William Charron, the late Ray Warren (who admitted Pronto driver #17 to Reed College), Liam Toomey, Doug Hommel, the brothers Malone, the brothers Galalis, the brothers Lieuallen, the brothers Rancher, the brothers McGee, John Hammond, Emily Brennan, Julianne Dolan, Shawn Sheehy, Rosanna Warren, Ted Frazier, Sanford Schwartz, Gregory Jones, Ronald Jay Robins, Maureen Matthews, Clayton Callope, Kevin Kraft, Kevin Jarvis, Thomas and Patricia Lawler, the late Carl Simpson, Shirley Adams, Joseph Nawrocki, S. P. Clarke, Lihui Liu, Robert Knapp of Reed College, Reverend Gary George and the patriarchs at noontime hoops, Knights of Columbus Council #13575, and Fathers Michael Bafaro, Robert Beloin, and Rocco Piccolomini. My mother, Maureen Waters, and my stepfather, David Kleinbard, have been most supportive. My errors are invariably my own.

I am indebted to my editors at the University of Missouri Press, Clair Willcox and Julianna Schroeder.

I thank The College of the Holy Cross for a grant that helped with the writing of this book. As always, the college's hardworking librarians came to my rescue. Special thanks (again) to Diana Antul.

THE RETURN OF
CHRISTIAN
HUMANISM

Part I

Humanism and Culture

1

Between Two Worlds

I begin with one of Eliot's more abstract formulations, a large gray bolus that will take the non-equine reader a moment to digest. The topic is the relation of poetry to belief. To explain this relation, Eliot engages two competing points of view. In the first case, if "you deny . . . that full poetic appreciation is possible without belief in what the poet believed, you deny the existence of 'poetry' as well as 'criticism'; and if you push this denial to its conclusion, you will be forced to admit that there is very little poetry that you can appreciate." In the second case, "if you yourself are convinced of a certain view of life, then you irresistibly and inevitably believe that if any one else comes to 'understand' it fully, his understanding must terminate in belief." Eliot comments that both views tend to become "heresies . . . not . . . in the theological, but in a more general sense." He continues, "Each is true only within a limited field of discourse, but unless you limit fields of discourse, you can have no discourse at all. Orthodoxy can only be found in such contradictions." This use of the word *orthodoxy* is closely related to Eliot's defense of humanism (from 1928) as that which "makes for breadth, tolerance, equilibrium and sanity." Humanism, says Eliot, "operates against fanaticism."[1] In Eliot's "more general sense," which is *paratheological* and not *atheological*, "orthodoxy" means "tolerance" in the republic of letters. It supports Eliot's ideal, reflected in his editorship of the *Criterion,* of a fresh movement of ideas among western artists and intellectuals.

As creative writers of genius, Chesterton, Eliot, and Tolkien are orthodox in this humanistic sense, leaving the reader to unfold their

---

1. T. S. Eliot, *Selected Essays,* 230, 436.

theological and metaphysical implications. As Christian apologists, they seek to "address non-Christians *on grounds that are acceptable to non-Christians.*"[2] Their works show flashes of sectarianism (some of Eliot's build into an artificial day), but they are widely admitted to the company of literary authors, writing in the western tradition, which is tolerant, accommodating, and meritocratic. As literary artists, they invite imaginative responses that are untouched by political and religious rancor. But the task is hard, and so they struggle always and characteristically with a precarious balance, which admits the contradictions between two fields of discourse, literature and belief.

Today's educational establishment bears a passing resemblance to Dionysius of Syracuse, whom Plato himself could not influence. In its worst moods, it has sacrificed the great minds to an enforced conformity. For the late Christopher Lasch, the problem was the tyrant's new clothes:

> "Diversity"—a slogan that looks attractive on the face of it—has come to mean the opposite of what it appears to mean. In practice, diversity turns out to legitimize a new dogmatism, in which rival minorities take shelter behind a set of beliefs impervious to rational discussion. . . . This parody of "community"—a term much in favor but not very clearly understood—carries with it the insidious assumption that all members of a given group can be expected to think alike.[3]

As Lasch understands it, diversity is not humanism. It is not an exchange of ideas. It is an administrative shell where a host of "rival minorities" have for the moment taken refuge. We can readily see, for instance, that there is no real discipline of diversity. There is no logic to "the diversity of groupthink." Going back to Eliot's humanistic concern with fields of discourse, we find the heretical thrust of diversity

---

2. Gavin D'Costa, *Theology in the Public Square: Church, Academy, and Nation,* 85.

3. Christopher Lasch, *The Revolt of the Elites and the Betrayal of Democracy,* 17–18. For the effects of diversity on U.S. campuses, see Donald Alexander Downs, *Restoring Free Speech and Liberty on Campus;* and Alan Charles Kors and Harvey A. Silvergate, *The Shadow University: The Betrayal of Liberty on America's Campuses.* For the effects of diversity on British education, see Melanie Phillips, *Londonistan,* 62–76.

is what holds it together. It attracts those, including some Christians, who deny that Christianity is culturally necessary. Lasch acknowledges the widespread suspicion "that religious tolerance . . . is a contradiction in terms." Along the same lines, George Marsden remarks that "radical feminists, lesbians, and gays . . . see traditional Christianity as one of the powers from which the world needs to be liberated." Both Lasch and Marsden recognize legitimate concerns about Christian intolerance. But it is typical of our contemporary confusion that the feminist who coos at the Koran finds western values to be threatening.[4] If diversity is a cover for intellectual chaos, while common sense suffocates in the vacuum of groupthink, then we need to give more thought to the Christian sources of tolerance in our lives.

The argument of this book is that Christian humanism conserves the radical middle between secularism and theocracy. The one extreme is the perversion of state power, the other is the perversion of religious power. I think that the biggest danger to western society comes from these power blocs, from the hate and fanaticism that they breed, and that there is an urgent need for dialogue.

Searching for the sources of free intellectual exchange and the life of the mind, we meet everywhere with partisans hunkered down in immoveable positions. There are no unifying figures. One side wants to secularize, the other to proselytize. Since I profess to be a Christian, I doubt that secularists will be persuaded by my saying that the potential threat from Christian theocracy is less real than they suppose. Even granting, which I do, that their vigilance is justified, I think the danger from radicalized Islam is more serious to western society than any danger currently posed by Christian zealotry. Ironically, though, Islam introduces another voice into a conversation that has already failed. Constructive dialogue between secular and religious fell apart well before the epoch-making events of September 11, 2001, and July 7, 2005. Over the length of this book, I hope to illuminate the causes behind our long cultural impasse, but what is immediately notable is that the breakdown of dialogue corresponds closely to the decline of humanism. The word itself has become almost uselessly equivocal.

4. Lasch, *Revolt,* 15; George M. Marsden, *The Outrageous Idea of Christian Scholarship,* 32. On cooing feminists, see, for example, Miriam Cooke, "Multiple Critique: Islamic Feminist Rhetorical Strategies."

Fortunately, there is no reason to cloister in some nostalgic period when humanism flourished, if we want to recover its meaning. Not to rush in blindly, but to approach the future consciously: that is what we want. And that means knowing the past.

What, then, was humanism? Inside that monument of spiritual marble known as the *Oxford English Dictionary*, we find the first entry under *humanism* to be an obsolete sense from the early nineteenth century: "Belief in the mere humanity of Christ." The illustrative quotation is from 1812. Wearing his theologian's cap, Samuel Taylor Coleridge describes a "man who has passed from orthodoxy to the loosest Arminianism, and thence to Arianism, and thence to direct Humanism." As a dissent from predestination, Arminian doctrine is liberalized Calvinism. To have preached Arminianism, like John Wesley, was to open salvation to all living souls, not only the elect. The "loosest Arminianism," of which Coleridge speaks, means that nobody is damned. Arianism is much older. It was condemned by the first Council of Nicaea (325) for denying the full divinity of Christ. Its elimination was crucial to the orthodox Church and encouraged a robust Trinitarianism in western Europe. Coleridge describes a process of spiritual decay, where perennial heresies adorn the path to atheism. Humanism makes its debut in a cautionary tale that ends with a man, if not mankind, bereft of hope. In a sense, we are back with the Ancient Mariner, "Alone on a wide wide sea: / So lonely 'twas, that God himself / Scarce seemed there to be."[5]

Only the faint ghost of religion survives in the *OED*'s second definition, which hinges on the word *devotion*: "The character or quality of being human; devotion to human interests." So used, *humanism* has little descriptive force. It is a decorative abstraction. All the quotations illustrating this definition share "an enlightened spirit of humanism" (1836), a breezy optimistic glow—as when William Ewart Gladstone flatters Hermes that he "exceeds in humanism . . . the other Olympian gods."

In definition three, the ghost perks up: "Any system of thought or action which is concerned with merely human interests (as distinguished from divine), or with those of the human race in general (as distinguished from individual); the 'Religion of Humanity.'" Gladstone, cited again,

5. Samuel Taylor Coleridge, *The Oxford Authors: Samuel Taylor Coleridge*, 65.

makes *humanism* a synonym for "Comtism or Positivism" (1876). The Comtean variety of humanism was warmly received by such leading English intellectuals as J. S. Mill and George Henry Lewes.[6] Positivism, the more purely scientific offspring of Comte, was adopted by Leslie Stephen, Samuel Butler, and T. H. Huxley; in the United States it would later be welcomed by John Dewey.[7] Comte can be grouped with two other utopian Frenchmen, Charles Fourier and Saint-Simon, "who claimed to have discovered the secret of social development" and who "became the founders of sects."[8] Scientist and prophet, coiner of the word *sociology,* Comte envisioned his positivist description of scientific laws to be the crowning achievement of history, an end to successive stages of religious and metaphysical superstition. Chesterton would jauntily describe the same scientific laws as inexplicable magic. Eric Voegelin would observe that Comte offered only "a hell of social oblivion" to souls who could not follow his scientific agenda. One of Comte's preoccupations was to smooth the transition from Catholicism to humanism. He replaced the feast days of Catholic saints with those of free thinkers like Adam Smith, Frederick the Great, and none other than August Comte himself as Supreme Pontiff. He thought the Cult of the Virgin, "under the gradual impulsion of the positivists, assisted by the women and the regenerate Jesuits," could prepare people for the coming of "our Goddess," Humanity.[9] Through Comte's influence, then, humanism became a conscious alternative to Christianity. The myth of progress, the Comtean calendar of great men, the worship of humanity: these were all recastings of the Catholic claim to supply meaning and purpose in life. To the moral-minded Victorian in reaction against mumbo-jumbo, humanism was revered as something "higher" and more "enlightened" than its orthodox rival.

Our fourth definition has a scholarly aura: "Devotion to those studies which promote human culture; literary culture; esp. the system of

6. For Comte's reception in England, see Walter E. Houghton, *The Victorian Frame of Mind.* For Comte and intellectual history, see J. B. Bury, *The Idea of Progress;* and Henri de Lubac, S.J., *The Drama of Atheist Humanism.*

7. For Comte and Dewey, see Marsden, *Outrageous Idea,* 26.

8. Bury, *Idea of Progress,* 278–79.

9. Eric Voegelin, *The New Science of Politics,* 107–32. See also Bury, *Idea of Progress,* 305–6; Comte quoted in de Lubac, *Drama of Atheist Humanism,* 117–18.

the Humanists, the study of the Roman and Greek classics which came into vogue at the Renascence." The rites of "devotion" persist. But here, most crucially, the relation between humanism and the "Religion of Humanity" is ambiguous. For centuries, to be a humanist had been to be a scholar. But the illustrative quotations for definition four, which begin in 1838, disclose a remarkable shift. The dictionary quotes Matthew Arnold's "Literature and Science," an important lecture from 1882: "We talk of knowing Greek and Roman antiquity . . . which is what people have called humanism." If we return to the original lecture, we find Arnold elaborating a distinction between "a superficial humanism," which is "mainly decorative" (one thinks of definition two), and a "genuine humanism," which is both literary and "scientific."[10] And when it turns out that the humanist's job description is to defend the instincts for religion and poetry against the overreach of science, we can see that Arnold takes Renaissance humanism in a bold new direction, more inviting to the poet than to the philologist.

Paul Oskar Kristeller, a noted authority on the subject, derives our modern understanding of humanism from the German *Humanismus*, coined by a German educator in 1808 "to express the emphasis on Greek and Latin classics in secondary education, as against the rising demands for a more practical and more scientific training."[11] Kristeller observes that humanism did not begin as a matter of doctrine:

> I should like to understand Renaissance humanism, at least in its origin and in its typical representatives, as a broad cultural and literary movement, which in its substance was not philosophical, but had important philosophical implications and consequences. I have been unable to discover in the humanist literature any common philosophical doctrine, except a belief in the value of man and the humanities and in the revival of ancient learning.[12]

The passage reflects the important point that the Renaissance had no humanism, per se. In the nineteenth century, humanism came into

---

10. Matthew Arnold, *Complete Prose Works,* 10:57.
11. Paul Oskar Kristeller, *Renaissance Thought: The Classic, Scholastic, and Humanist Strains,* 9.
12. Ibid., 22.

being, and "humanist literature" became "humanistic."[13] C. S. Lewis, while blasting the pedantry of much Renaissance humanism, reaches a similar verdict about the Renaissance: "'Humanists' in the modern sense hardly existed."[14] But if humanists in the modern sense hardly existed, is the existence of humanism over the centuries just a case of what philosophers call reification, an illusion fostered by the invention of the noun *humanism*? Or can we discover more persuasive if subterranean continuities among the humanists?

There is such a thing as sharing a definite doctrine, and there is such as thing, observed by Goethe, as elective affinity. It is certainly true that the Renaissance humanists did not champion what Erasmus poetically called "the third church" (neither Catholic nor Lutheran) as a doctrinal alternative.[15] And yet there is a peculiar thread of continuity in the story of humanism that deserves attention, because it is one of those small parts that is vital to our understanding of the whole. In an essay on Addison, Lewis offers the following prejudicial but intelligent remark about the Renaissance humanists:

> Learning to them meant the knowledge and imitation of a few rather arbitrarily selected Latin authors and some even fewer Greek authors. They despised metaphysics and natural science; and they despised all the past outside their favoured periods. They were dominated by a narrowly ethical purpose . . . in Erasmus, in Rabelais, in the *Utopia* one recognizes the very accent of the angry *belle-lettrist* railing, as he rails in all ages, at "jargon" and "straw-splitting." On this side Pope and Swift are true inheritors of the Humanist tradition.[16]

Erasmus was among the most learned men in Europe: it is hard to find anything narrow about him at all.[17] But Lewis is right that humanist writers, from Erasmus to Swift, disliked the dagger definitions of

---

13. The *OED* supports this distinction. Interestingly, two of the entries under *humanistic* come from Walter Pater.

14. C. S. Lewis, *English Literature in the Sixteenth Century,* 18.

15. See Paul Johnson, *A History of Christianity,* 279.

16. C. S. Lewis, "Addison," quoted in Jenny Mezciems, "Swift's Praise of Gulliver: Some Renaissance Background to the *Travels,*" 246.

17. See Louis Bouyer, *Erasmus and His Times,* in itself an excellent introduction to Christian humanism.

theology. They wrote in reaction against moldy scholasticism, rabid sectarianism, and all the ways that theology can abuse reason and incite bloodshed. To a humanistic sensibility, Erasmus is more congenial than Luther, but Luther saw deeper in one great respect, for he understood (what many intellectuals overlook) that theology cannot simply be brushed aside. He knew that the question of justification, for instance, was of immense concern to ordinary people. Renaissance humanism either failed to see or refused to admit any point in metaphysical rigor and theological disputation. And this defect is striking in two tragic acts played out by humanism before Chesterton: the first is that its essentially peaceful spirit, erudition, and love of truth almost succeeded in making the Reformation unnecessary. The second is that it ended in unbelief.

Tracing the origins of humanism back to the *litterae humaniores* ("the more humane letters") of Petrarch's revolt against the schoolmen, Jacques Barzun summarizes what is strong and positive in the humanist's endeavor. Yet his words ring differently than they would have back in Lewis's or Kristeller's day: "If we look for what is common to the Humanists over the centuries," Barzun writes, "we find two things: a body of accepted authors and a method of carrying on study and debate. The two go together with the belief that the best guides to the good life are Reason and Nature." Barzun might have been remembering Swift's exalted Houyhnhnms, who "thought Nature and Reason were sufficient Guides for a reasonable Animal."[18] The case for humanism has never been easy, and it is notable that both Kristeller and Barzun employ the word *belief.* A "belief in the value of man," in the context of the Martin Classical Lectures at Oberlin College in 1954, would not have raised many eyebrows. No doubt the experience of the Second World War lingered on people's nerves: Kristeller could not simply assume the value of man as a self-evident fact. On the other hand, "belief in the value of man" was not controversial, threatening the decorum of the faculty room and the future of the liberal arts. "Man" was not yet an outlaw, banned in the faculty statutes by a revolutionary act of social engineering. There were many living, breathing humanists holding down academic posts. By the end of the century, however, this

18. Jacques Barzun, *From Dawn to Decadence: 1500 Years of Western Cultural Life, 1500 to the Present,* 45–46; Jonathan Swift, *Gulliver's Travels,* 210.

was no longer the case. Barzun, who devotes several fine pages to defending the usage of *man,* describes a belief in abstract entities, Reason and Nature, that are alien to the postmodern mood. What was once common currency had lost its cash-value for all but a few.

As the twentieth century raced to a close, humanism collapsed like some brilliant nightmare out of Swift. Our species seemed abruptly to have altered, from *animal rationale* or even *animal rationis capax* (an animal capable of reason), to just another *animal.*[19] Darwin, the author of a theory that belongs in every ninth-grade biology class, was seized by anti-Christian writers and Christian fundamentalists alike, who used him as a wedge to divide the culture in two. Both sides were, and continue to be, insular and narrow-minded. In this case of cultural fragmentation, as in many others, the humanist is called upon to engage religion and science, and to combine tolerance with good judgment. But the doctor is too sick to get off the couch.

Western man has become darkly obsessed with past failure. A spirit of repentance has changed, over the course of one or two generations, into a massive cultural trauma. We have grown very skillful at denouncing our heroes, our churches, our canons of art, our metaphysics, our past, and our future. In this respect, we are consuming our seed corn as we weep over our plates. We have developed in our compassionate selves, to great quivering flourishes of sympathy, all kinds of morbid tastes, including a taste for the salt of our own tears. We have settled into gross habits of materialism, which we dignify with weightless prizes and meaningless words (for example, "academic excellence"). The current crisis is exacerbated by chilling demographic tables and morally problematic advances in biology. Losing the will to be human, we are witnessing the birth of the posthuman.[20]

This hour was long in coming. It is the unhappy orphan of humanism, which, as we have seen, developed in the Victorian period, when science was routing theology from the universities, before Tolstoy and Nietzsche meditated on the limits of science, before electronic technology made its transformative impact known, and before Christianity discovered the historical and imaginative means to defend itself. It is

19. With a nod to Swift (the famous 1725 letter to Pope). See *Gulliver's Travels,* 262.

20. For this possibility, see Francis Fukuyama, *Our Posthuman Future: Consequences of the Biotechnology Revolution.*

Arnoldian liberal humanism that most concerns us, for Arnold set in play a series of actions and reactions that show why humanism is necessary and why it was lost.

Born in 1822, Matthew Arnold was the son of the famous Rugby headmaster, the Reverend Thomas Arnold, who led the Broad Church opposition to Cardinal Newman. Matt played the dandy at Oxford, where he took a Second Class degree, the result, as one critic colorfully remarks, "of too diligent attention to fishing and French novels."[21] Later he fell in with a fashionable crowd in Paris, and pursued a French actress. But after his father's early death, which is movingly remembered in the poem "Rugby Chapel," he inherited the family mantle as educator and moralist. For thirty-five years he worked as a school inspector in England and Wales, a career he managed to balance with family, poetry, and criticism.

Arnold was in many respects a late product of Renaissance humanism, not only because of his exuberant classicism, his work on curriculum reform, and his satirical thrust and parry, but also because a streak of urbane skepticism led him to dismiss metaphysics and theology. Arnold saw himself as a liminal figure, "Wandering between two worlds, one dead, / The other powerless to be born."[22] But if Arnold was a liminal figure, it is not because western consciousness was wandering, as he imagined, between medieval Christendom and a promised land founded on culture and the cosmic order. Arnold was liminal for a different reason. He came at the end of the tradition of Renaissance humanism that runs from Erasmus through Swift and Pope; and he wrote the prologue to the Christian humanism that begins anew with Chesterton.

Persuaded that Christianity was doomed by science, Arnold sought to replace religion with culture. Like Eliot, many Christians therefore find it difficult to appreciate Arnold's strengths. This is unfortunate, because Arnold is indispensable. Unlike his father, he expressed considerable admiration for Newman, whose writings on liberal education form the background for his educational initiatives. He broadens the application of Newman's ideas, and he is immensely useful to Christian apologists who follow him in the field of culture, even as his

21. *Poetry and Criticism of Matthew Arnold,* xxi.
22. Matthew Arnold, "Stanzas from the Grande Chartreuse" (lines 85–86), in *The Poems of Matthew Arnold,* 302.

agnosticism suggests the need, which Newman keenly recognized, for religious authority.

Arnold established liberal humanism on the basis of human nature, which he approached through the Aristotelian question, *What are the grounds of human flourishing?* This is not to say that he endorsed a metaphysics of potentiality and act; his care for Reason and Nature was based on his sense of culture and the good life. His humanism is basically consistent with the definition given by Jacques Maritain, that humanism "tends to render man more truly human and to make his original greatness manifest by causing him to participate in all that can enrich him in nature and in history." For both Arnold and Maritain, "humanism is inseparable from civilisation and culture." Likewise, Pope John Paul II identifies humanism with culture, "that through which man, as man, becomes more man, 'is' more." Nations, he argues, have a right to "the humanistic perspective of man's development."[23] In his defense of culture, Arnold expounded the classics, execrated Americanization, and exercised "Darwin's bulldog," the highly formidable T. H. Huxley, in the lecture I have briefly quoted, "Literature and Science." Arnold debated Huxley on the comparative importance of humanism and science. He confronted Huxley with a humanistic synthesis of science, morality, and art (that is, truth, goodness, and beauty); the technical scientist, he said, lacked this capacity for relating distant ideas and satisfying human nature.

Fearing a breakdown of social order, Arnold tried to protect Victorian England from some of its coarsest elements: anarchists, utilitarians, and hidebound Puritans. He tried to steer the English away from a crabbed insularity, to bring them closer to the continent. "Arnold was not only right but highly valuable," wrote Chesterton, who lauded Arnold's approach to modern democracy, from his insistence on "a rational minimum of culture and common courtesy" to his appreciation of small business ownership.[24] In *Culture and Anarchy,* Arnold diagnosed the mid-Victorian crisis. He concentrated on the English reception of two traditions, Hebraism and Hellenism, with the former dominating in the lives of middle-class Puritans. He built a strong case for expanding the Greek contribution, which he called

---

23. Jacques Maritain, *True Humanism,* xii; John Paul II, *Memory and Identity: Conversations at the Dawn of the Millennium,* 85.

24. G. K. Chesterton, *The Victorian Age in Literature,* 74.

(by way of Swift) "sweetness and light." He certainly did not want to discard its Hebraic, religious counterpart, but he could not reconcile the Bible and science. And so, having refused religious dogma, he turned for foundations to a quasi-religious faith in the saving power of poetry. "The future of poetry is immense," he wrote.[25] It was not the worst prophecy uttered in Victorian England—not when Karl Marx was in business. But Arnold estranged both the Christian and the aesthete, who found him neither inspiring nor credible. He was too heretical for one and too earnest for the other.

I have so far omitted from consideration a lengthy, fifth (and final) definition of *humanism* from the *OED*, which may be summarized as "the humanism of William James." Writing in 1904, James uses the term to denote a "wider pragmatism" covering "the notion that the truth of any statement *consists* in the consequences, and particularly their being good consequences." James and Arnold are intellectual congeners, and Arnold uses the term *pragmatic* in just this sense of attention to "consequences." James, however, was more religious than Arnold. The leader of the pragmatist school considered himself to be a Christian, and though he was not sectarian, he was rigorously independent. He writes: "I myself read humanism theistically and pluralistically. . . . If there be a God, he is no absolute all-experiencer, but simply the experiencer of widest conscious span. Read thus, humanism is for me a religion susceptible of reasoned defence." James's argument for the soul, his insights into mystical experience, his quest for God, are touchstones of existential belief. But he could not dispel the spiritual confusion that humanism generated. By his own admission, his humanism looked like Kantian idealism. It therefore lent itself more to rationalization than to reason. More generally, pragmatism fails in the role of humanism for reasons that Comte foresaw: it starves the soul. To quote the author of *Ulysses* on the work of a leading Jamesian humanist, it lacks a depth of "humane insight."[26] For mind-food, Joyce preferred Thomism: it was just more interesting.

25. Arnold, *Complete Prose Works,* 9:161.

26. William James, *Writings, 1902–1910,* 857; Jacques Barzun, *A Stroll with William James,* 90n; James, *Writings, 1902–1910,* 891–92; James Joyce, *The Critical Writings,* 135.

The backlash against Arnold began in 1873, when Walter Pater published his *Studies in the History of the Renaissance*. The leader of the aesthetic movement was a shy homosexual who grew alarmed at his own success.[27] Highly learned in classics and philosophy (especially German philosophy), he spent most of his life at Oxford, where he tutored the young Gerard Manley Hopkins. His deathbed conversion to the Church of Rome foreshadows the conversions of two writers who took his aestheticism much to heart: Oscar Wilde and Wallace Stevens. The Catholic Pater is almost entirely forgotten; otherwise, it might be argued that aestheticism has always benefited from a Christian refinement of feeling, from an intimate and feminine receptivity, for which the life of Saint Mary Magdalene is archetype and paragon. Today it is the fashion to place Pater in the avant-garde, as a genius who unshackled the mind. Whatever truth this view might hold, it rests on the shifting grounds of progress. Certainly Pater exerted a great deal of influence, but his work did not have the kind of constructive moral impact that he intended. The reasons for Pater's failure as a moralist have to do with the limits of aestheticism; but the success of aestheticism has to do with the crisis in European politics. I am not sure whether Pater grasped the nature of his timing. What happened was that his peculiar approach to the Renaissance suited the growing skepticism of later generations toward the established order. He offered the solace of beauty, and a retreat from the unrelenting blunders of civilization.

According to Chesterton, the black year of 1870 was "the turn of the century." In a passage whose prophetic intensity has not waned, he sums up the discontent of Europe as modernity took its unpredictable course. It is a passage that adamantly resists abbreviation:

> About 1870 the force of the French Revolution faltered and fell: the year that was everywhere the death of Liberal ideas: the year when Paris fell: the year when Dickens died. While the new foes of freedom, the sceptics and scientists, were damaging democracy in ideas, the old foes of freedom, the emperors and kings, were damaging her more heavily in arms. For a moment it almost seemed that the old Tory ring of iron, the Holy Alliance, had recombined against France. But there was just this difference: that the Holy Alliance was now not

27. For Pater's homoeroticism, see James Najarian, *Victorian Keats: Manliness, Sexuality, and Desire,* 136–60.

arguably, but almost avowedly, an Unholy Alliance. It was an alliance
between those who still thought they could deny the dignity of man
and those who had recently begun to have a bright hope of denying
even the dignity of God. Eighteenth century Prussia was Protestant
and probably religious. Nineteenth century Prussia was almost utterly
atheist. Thus the old spirit of liberty felt itself shut up at both ends,
that which was called progressive and that which was called reactionary: barricaded by Bismarck with blood and iron and by Darwin
by blood and bones. The enormous depression which infects many
excellent people born about this time, probably has this cause.[28]

These depressed and excellent people (among whom we may place
Chesterton himself) were the radical middle of their day, caught
between false progress and real reaction. I infer that they included liberal Catholics. In 1870 the dogma of papal infallibility issued from
the Vatican amid populist fanfare. Pope Pius IX, the force behind the
antidemocratic "Syllabus of Errors," succeeded in silencing or dispir-
iting liberal Catholics throughout Europe, men like Lord Acton in
England, his close friend Professor Johann von Dollinger in Germany,
and Bishop Doupanloup in France. It was little consolation that Pius
was one of the few European leaders able to stand up to Bismarck.
England, to its credit, never followed Prussia, Russia, and Austria in
the Holy Alliance of 1815, and after 1870 the conservative reaction
in England was comparatively gentle. Disraeli continued a policy of
social reform when he became prime minister in 1874, changing the
tone of conservative politics and adjusting the upper classes to democracy. But the new imperialism poisoned the politics of England,
Germany, and the United States, corrupted the Church, and spread
like a stain throughout Europe.

It was in this historical milieu that the aesthetic movement crip-
pled—and then mocked—the public spirit of Arnoldian liberal
humanism. This reaction is inscribed in such key modernist texts as
Ulysses, and Eliot in his later attacks on Arnold echoes some of Wilde's
jeers, as does Marxist critic Terry Eagleton in his critique of liberal
humanism.[29] Bloomsbury likewise sided with Pater. Here I want to

28. Chesterton, *Victorian Age,* 213–14.
29. Eagleton writes that liberal humanism "is at once perfectly reasonable
and . . . entirely useless" (Terry Eagleton, *Literary Theory: An Introduction,* 210).

underscore the point that Pater did not actually reject humanism; he revised it. Pater's humanism is mannerist—romantic and decadent. His intellectual landscape has Reason and Nature falling under the sway of Schopenhauer and Darwin. His "refined and comely decadence," which appears in his work as a reverie of the lives of famous artists and humanists, proves on examination to be a series of veiled self-portraits whose author treasured in his heart a gloomy determinism. He preached the "hard, gemlike flame" of aesthetic freedom,[30] but devotees caught the whisper of a terrible secret, the erotic spellbinding of fate, after which Arnold's earnestness sounded like crude parental moralizing.

Though Arnold inspired reaction in the most important modernist writers, liberal humanism mingled with modernism because the universities maintained an intense interest in western culture. Arnold made his greatest impact among educators, including such luminaries as Charles Eliot Norton, Irving Babbitt, I. A. Richards, F. R. Leavis, Lionel Trilling, and Walter Jackson Bate. For a time, the noble practice of highbrow liberal humanism flourished in their sensitive writings.[31] The miraculous example of Eliot as poet, critic, and playwright breathed new life into the canon and critical standards. At the same time, liberal humanism catered to the post-Christian religious needs of English professors, many of whom taught one version or another of the Arnoldian creed that poetry can save us. That is chiefly what Eliot meant in 1933, when he told the students at Harvard University, "Examination of the criticism of our time leads me to believe that we are still in Arnold's period."[32] Arnold's influence eventually waned due to a host of factors. The professoriate succumbed to "science envy," which tainted the formalistic readings of the New Criticism, preparing the academy for deconstruction. The antihumanist element in modernism gathered strength among critical heirs influenced by literary theory, much of it aesthetic in origin. Canon wars, the long Renaissance battle over who belongs in the body of accepted authors, raged with

30. Walter Pater, *Works*, 1:xii–xiii, 236.
31. Among contemporary critics, few acknowledge Arnold's influence. Two notable exceptions are Morris Dickstein, *Double Agent: The Critic and Society*, 8–34; and Christopher Ricks, introduction to *The Oxford Book of English Verse*.
32. T. S. Eliot, *The Use of Poetry and the Use of Criticism*, 121.

creative ferocity until the modernists died off. The canon itself was shelved by 1990, by which time the professors were in thrall to anti-humanism and no longer cared to preserve a tradition. The critical method was madness by 1996, when Alan Sokal hoaxed a leading scholarly journal. Sokal's piece of sublime nonsense was called "Transgressing the Boundaries: Toward a Transformative Hermeneutics of Quantum Gravity." The journal's editors, with the Reason and Nature that distinguished them, rejected Sokal's explanatory follow-up essay "on the grounds that it did not meet their intellectual standards."[33] By the end of the twentieth century, liberal humanism was in the discount bin.

By comparison, the end of the nineteenth century did not witness the entire collapse of humanism, but it was a period touched by considerable anxiety in intellectual circles. The imperialist was bloodied, the clergyman weak, the scientist all but unaccountable. Wilde pinned the Green Carnation on his lapel, in elegant defiance of the sinister trap laid by nature and reason (it would take Atlas to sustain the capitals).[34] The new press, armed with foreign correspondents and telegraphs, stimulated a quicker, less stable movement of public opinion. The masses had begun their slow, unsteady climb to a better life. Progress had been made but leadership was poor. With the passing of the immensely popular Victoria, the *Times* of London editorialized, "the impetus has to some extent spent itself."[35] Somehow out of this smoke and fog emerged the most gifted defender of Christian humanism since Erasmus. I speak, of course, of Chesterton.

33. Alan Sokal and Jean Bricmont, *Fashionable Nonsense: Postmodern Intellectuals' Abuse of Science,* 268.
34. Insects will not pollinate the green flower.
35. Quoted in G. M. Young, *Victorian England: Portrait of an Age,* 157.

Part II

THREE CHRISTIAN HUMANISTS

2

G. K. CHESTERTON (1874–1936)

Gilbert Keith Chesterton was born in Kensington to highly respectable, nominally Christian parents. He was always at home in the suburbs. At the age of twenty-seven, he settled into a happy marriage, though his wife was never able to bear children.[1] There is something of a parallel with Eliot. Like Vivienne Haigh-Wood, Frances Blogg was an attractive young woman with a literary bent. It is quite possible that neither of the two couples consummated their marriage during their honeymoons. Both women suffered from acute physical debilities. But that is where the parallel ends. Chesterton was sexually healthier than Eliot; and Gilbert and Frances were by all reports devoted to each other until death. Unlike poor Vivienne, Frances brought her husband the consoling gift of intense Anglo-Catholic faith.

In his early years, Chesterton grappled with demons who were frighteningly intelligent. His lips tasted the witches' brew of Schopenhauer, his nerves suffered the hammer blows of materialism, his mind foundered in a sea of doubt. But there may be something to Emerson's stodgy apothegm: "In general, every evil to which we do not succumb is a benefactor."[2] The career of Chesterton stands as a victory for humankind. It represents the last major victory over cosmic despair, which menaces our own period in the form of antihumanism.

Recovering from his personal Victorian crisis, Chesterton learned to defend his humanistic faith in reason and nature *as a faith*. He was not the first to make this argument. F. H. Bradley preceded him in commenting that philosophy rests on an act of faith. Nietzsche wondered

---

1. See Michael Ffinch, *G. K. Chesterton: A Biography*, 97–98.
2. *The Selected Writings of Ralph Waldo Emerson*, 184.

if modern science might be an evasion of truth. But Chesterton approached these ideas with ordinary people in mind. He informed a wide readership that history was entering a new phase, and he observed the terms and consequences of the shift. "Reason," he explained, "is itself a matter of faith. It is an act of faith to assert that our thoughts have any relation to reality at all."[3] Chesterton's job, then, was to make ordinary people aware that common sense, if it was going to survive the twentieth century, needed a religious foundation.

The Edwardians shared the Victorians' enthusiasm for the field of debate, where Chesterton cultivated the Christian soil that was lying fallow. Arnold, in his secular wisdom, had defined the activity of criticism as *a disinterested endeavour to learn and propagate the best that is known and thought in the world.*[4] Chesterton accepted the humanistic part of this argument, but he was less "disinterested":

> To know the best theories of existence and to choose the best from them (that is, to the best of our own strong conviction) appears to us the proper way to be neither bigot nor fanatic, but . . . a man with a definite opinion. But that definite opinion must in this view begin with the basic matters of human thought, and these must not be dismissed as irrelevant, as religion, for instance, is too often in our days dismissed as irrelevant.[5]

In a world of bigots and fanatics (the world of Arnold's *Culture and Anarchy*), disinterestedness might encourage agreement among a select few who share the same background and general outlook. But if you really want a democracy, Chesterton argues, you cannot ignore the need for a "theory of the cosmos," in which every citizen has a great deal at stake. It is a matter of our being equipped to live life freely and well: "The most practical and important thing about a man is still his view of the universe." Chesterton reposes considerable trust in the ordinary person as the real custodian of democracy. In this way he resembles Whitman, whom he admired and saw as an antidote to Schopenhauer and to aestheticism (I will discuss Schopenhauer in Chapter 5).

3. G. K. Chesterton, *Collected Works,* 1:236. The sad truth is that some volumes of this timely and useful edition of Chesterton are corrupt.

4. Arnold, *Complete Prose Works,* 3:283.

5. Chesterton, *Collected Works,* 1:203–4.

Democracy means personal responsibility in the realm of ideas, that we should "be steeped in philosophy and soaked in religion."[6] Chesterton's point is not just that faith and reason go together. It is that without a coherent view of the world, we will be left with chaos.

With prophetic boldness, Chesterton warned against the "great silent collapse" of civilization. In Arnold's spiritual resignation, he heard a death-knell in the West. He argued that Arnold's skepticism ("'miracles do not happen'") was itself only a new form of dogma, a "simple faith." It was curious that this faith could masquerade as truth, for Chesterton knew (he might have taken the lesson from Hume) that in the "science of physical facts . . . there are no laws, but only weird repetitions."[7] The mesmerizing authority of laws that do not exist was one instance of the chronic fatigue that Chesterton saw everywhere: in the mindless cant about progress, in the yellow press, in the pseudo-scientific jargon of modernizing scholarship, including the "higher criticism." There is a sense in Chesterton's work that he is accusing his countrymen of sloth, the capital sin of acedia, a type of depression understood by Christian writers as lethargy, apathy, and virtues left to drift. That is not a bad way of describing England in the 1890s. Chesterton learned from Nietzsche's analysis of European decay, especially, I think, from Zarathustra's comments on the shameless "last men," sheeplike worshippers of success.[8] But he detected in Nietzsche a flaw that Nietzscheans like George Bernard Shaw and William Butler Yeats overlooked: he saw in all those fascinating pages the fastidiousness of the hypersensitive. Nietzsche's apotheosis of power betrayed his secret weakness. To Chesterton's practiced eye, Nietzsche was an aesthete in wolf's clothing.

Chesterton reacted with a fierce apostasy against the aesthetic movement, for he was deeply influenced by Wilde's use of paradox, and, like Yeats, chose art school over a traditional university education. His answer to the "hard, gemlike flame" of Pater was to defend human nature: "There is only one way in which passions can become hard and gem-like, and that is by becoming cold as gems. No blow . . . has ever been struck at the natural loves and laughter of men so sterilizing as

6. Ibid., 1:41, 203.
7. Ibid., 1:51, 331, 254.
8. Friedrich Nietzsche, *Thus Spoke Zarathustra: A Book for All and None*, 16–19.

this *carpe diem* of the aesthetes." By isolating discrete moments in the flux of time, Pater attained a frozen perfection. But he robbed man of the continuity through time where his nature achieves its fullest expression. For Chesterton, our existence "is a story." Chesterton's appeal to narrative is philosophically profound; at the same time, it reminds us that he is a novelist. He pays attention to the practical faith, in free will, in the liveability of life, that inspires the best modern fiction. "A man has control over many things in life," Chesterton writes; "he has control over enough things to be the hero of a novel."[9] Pater wrote a veiled genre of autobiography that he called "imaginary portraits"—finely woven reveries of impressions, memories, and desires. Chesterton wrote novels whose acrobatic heroes piece together their lives through moral acts, which restore friendship and community.

As a Christian apologist, the Chesterton of *Heretics* acknowledges the merits of those, preeminently Shaw, who engage the public on the level of ideas. He then turns the tables on his opponents, a formidable array of "heretics" including Pater, Nietzsche, Wilde, Shaw, Kipling, Wells, Tolstoy, Whistler, and Yeats. He makes them unwitting actors in his own central demonstration that Christianity alone furnishes a broad enough basis for social progress. None of the heretics can supply such a basis. Typically, their defects arise from a bad use of history and a false idea of human nature. Unpersuaded by Nietzsche's transvaluation of all values, which tried to make new angels of old devils, Chesterton maintained that progress could not occur when cultural ideals were constantly evolving; if the goal altered substantially, it could never be reached. Hence the Shavian religion of the Superman, of "a new god in the unimaginable future," was an impossible ideal, an inhuman project for humanity.[10]

The alienation of reason and nature, the absence of a cosmic theory, and a general failure of nerve, had transformed London into a New Babel, characterized by perspectivism. Truth had abandoned a whole that could no longer be stated. As Chesterton pointed out, Shaw, Kipling, Wells, and the others were said to represent "aspects of truth."[11] To the public at large, this jostling multitude of aspects was

---

9. Chesterton, *Collected Works,* 1:95, 143, 144.
10. Ibid., 1:67.
11. Ibid., 1:200.

as mad as Piccadilly Circus. It was some solace that perspectivism achieved dazzling effects in art. Conrad's *Heart of Darkness* influenced Chesterton's *Man Who Was Thursday,* and the brilliant nightmare of Picasso was close at hand. Chesterton's usual answer to perspectivism is the answer that realists have given to nominalists since the Middle Ages. We cannot know truth in its aspects unless we already have real knowledge of truth. But in the peroration of *Heretics* Chesterton regards the fate of truth from a modern standpoint, and he tries to move mountains, to shift the philosophical crisis from twilight to dawn. Like the fireworks that he loved, the passage soars into the heights, bursting from climax to breathless climax:

> We who are Christians never knew the great philosophic common sense which inheres in that mystery until the anti-Christian writers pointed it out to us. The great march of mental destruction will go on. Everything will be denied. Everything will become a creed. It is a reasonable position to deny the stones in the street; it will become a religious dogma to assert them. It is a rational thesis that we are all in a dream; it will be a mystical sanity to say that we are all awake. Fires will be kindled to testify that two and two make four. Swords will be drawn to prove that leaves are green in summer. We shall be left defending, not only the incredible virtues and sanities of human life, but something more incredible still, this huge impossible universe that stares us in the face. We shall fight for visible prodigies as if they were invisible. We shall look on the impossible grass and the skies with a strange courage. We shall be of those who have seen and yet have believed.[12]

In a sense we are left floating in the air, with the earth lost to our feet, buoyed only by faith. No longer a ready foundation, common sense after the anti-Christian turn becomes a "creed," threatened by less humanistic creeds, which usurp reason and reality. What Chesterton calls "the great march of mental destruction" is the fragmentation of modern thought. He foresaw the results and knew they would lead to religious conflict. *It is a reasonable position to deny the stones in the street:* Dr. Johnson refuted Bishop Berkeley by kicking a stone, but the psychology of subject and object dissolved the common pavements. *Fires*

12. Ibid., 1:206–7.

will be kindled to testify that two and two make four: the coincidence of thought and reality is the glory not of man but of God. *We shall be left defending, not only the incredible virtues and sanities of human life, but something more incredible still, this huge impossible universe that stares us in the face:* cut off from their supernatural source, reason and nature were gradually exiled by the Enlightenment, by the reaction against the Enlightenment, by the Decadence. The same world that Kant thought he had preserved as man's distinct realm of freedom, Schopenhauer invaded like a bad dream, which Wilde converted into farce.

What Chesterton proposes, then, is the rebuilding of humanistic confidence on the orthodox planks of the Apostles' Creed. He defends orthodoxy, in his 1908 book of that name, as a serendipitous truth with a deep personal element: "I will not call it my philosophy; for I did not make it. God and humanity made it; and it made me." Orthodoxy is said to answer a "double spiritual need . . . for that mixture of the familiar and the unfamiliar which Christendom has rightly named romance." It follows that romance assumes a place for mysticism, "that man can understand everything by the help of what he does not understand."[13] The degree to which our knowledge must rely on the help of what we do not understand is not a pressing issue today, but it was for Chesterton's generation. To take two prominent cases, Bertrand Russell, the scientific philosopher,[14] is diametrically opposed to Yeats, the mystical poet. In this setting, Chesterton's synthesis of faith and reason occupies a middle ground between two dogmatic epistemologies: godless scientism and occult mysticism.

Chesterton also pursued the problem of knowledge through his historical consciousness. *Orthodoxy* is, at its most profound, a romance of history, in which mankind is ontologically negated by modern heresy and skepticism, only to be restored to being through a fuller knowledge and appreciation of dogma. Pragmatism supplies the most relevant example of our historical self-negation, but we must take a somewhat roundabout approach to appreciate Chesterton's position.

In *Orthodoxy,* Chesterton pledges his allegiance to democracy: "I . . . have always believed in democracy, in the elementary liberal doctrine of a self-governing humanity." This admission of belief is (if you will)

13. Ibid., 1:211, 212, 231.
14. See, for example, Bertrand Russell, *Mysticism and Logic.*

a gentle counterpoint to Jefferson, whose belief in "the Laws of Nature and Nature's God" extended to "self-evident" truths. The America of Jefferson and Lincoln marked, for Chesterton, the "highest point of democratic idealism and conviction."[15] But the erosion of democratic faith and the erosion of religious faith turned out to be linked. "Exactly what gives its real dignity to the figure of Lincoln," Chesterton writes in *What I Saw in America,*

> is that he stands invoking a primitive first principle of the age of innocence, and holding up the tables of an ancient law, *against* the trend of the nineteenth century; repeating, "We hold these truths to be self-evident; that all men were created equal, being endowed by their creator, etc.," to a generation that was more and more disposed to say something like this: "We hold these truths to be probable enough for the pragmatists; that all things looking like men were evolved somehow, being endowed by heredity and environment with no equal rights, but very unequal wrongs," and so on.[16]

Chesterton admires Lincoln as a type of Moses, prefiguring the romance of history, and all that is at stake in crossing the modern wilderness. By contrast, the withering gaze of the skeptic insists that nothing is self-evident. The withering gaze of Darwin insists that all men are created unequally. The pragmatist takes the new intellectual landscape in stride, but it is not the promised land, a place where republican democracy can thrive.

If we cannot assert that truth is self-evident, but we want common sense, then pragmatism points in the right direction. "I agree with the pragmatists," Chesterton writes, "that apparent objective truth is not the whole matter; that there is an authoritative need to believe the things that are necessary to the human mind. But I say that one of those necessities is a belief in objective truth." Dewey scoffed at Chesterton, saying that he "spills the personal milk in the [philosopher's] cocoanut." That is, he plays into the pragmatist's hands. In Louis Menand's lucid exposition of Dewey, Chesterton confirms "what the pragmatist has always claimed, which is that people believe to be true just what they think it is good to believe to be true." For Dewey, Chesterton has

15. Chesterton, *Collected Works,* 1:249, 21:255.
16. Ibid., 21:258–59.

"already conceded the main point, which is that every account of the way people think is, at bottom, a support for those human goods the person making the account believes to be important."[17]

I am willing to concede that Dewey has won Dewey's point, but I think he has missed Chesterton's entirely. The pragmatist's argument stands on one condition: we must accept that "human goods" are entirely a matter of what "the person making the account believes to be important." We must handle "human goods" with quotation marks. We are theoretically detached to the point that we can prescind the goods of bread, milk, and a loving mother. So, for instance, we can abstain from certain hard moral judgments when it comes to the global economy: "A given culture reveals its overall understanding of life through the choices it makes in production and consumption."[18] It is interesting how this remark by John Paul II collapses into formal abstraction when viewed by a Deweyan. If you say, "every account of the way people think is, at bottom, a support for those human goods the person making the account believes to be important," I will say, "what gives you the authority to judge any account of human goods *qua* good? How do I know you are even talking about goods? Maybe you are just talking about what you think is important." In this decisive respect, pragmatism unmakes reality. It effectively annihilates the human as such, reducing man to a self-interested flux.

Chesterton's romance of history turns on his realization that Christian theology defines European culture against its rivals. While therapists touted innumerable bizarre fads in health and nutrition, Chesterton quoted the Sermon on the Mount: "Take no thought what ye shall eat or what ye shall drink, or wherewithal ye shall be clothed. For after all these things do the Gentiles seek. But seek first the kingdom of God and His righteousness, and all these things shall be added unto you."[19] While Pater's interest in reincarnation inspired a host of aesthetes,[20] Chesterton saw frightening social consequences in such flirtations: "The truth is that the western theology that dethrones tyrants has been directly due to the western theology that says 'I am

17. Ibid., 1:239; Louis Menand, "An Introduction to Pragmatism," xii.

18. John Paul II, *Centesimus Annus,* section 36.

19. Chesterton, *Collected Works,* 1:113.

20. For a sign of the times, see W. B. Yeats, introduction to *The Oxford Book of Modern Verse, 1892–1935,* xxx.

I, thou art thou.'" The Apostles' Creed, which is "the best root of energy and sound ethics," entails a fine theological balance. "Take away the Nicene Creed and similar things," he writes, "and you do some strange wrong to the sellers of sausages." And it is not only the sausage vendors who stand to lose. With respect to the historic councils, "A sentence phrased wrong about the nature of symbolism would have broken all the best statues in Europe. A slip in the definitions might stop all the dances; might wither all the Christmas trees or break all the Easter eggs."[21] Chesterton took seriously the theological boundaries that divide Rome from Byzantium, Christian from Muslim from Jew.

This habit of mind, though consistent with Chesterton's dislike of imperialism, cannot recommend him where multiculturalism is enshrined as the highest value. At his most problematic, he brandishes theology's sharp edge. He is militant, but he claims the right of cultural self-defense: "The truth is that Islam itself was a barbaric reaction against that very humane complexity that is really a Christian character; that idea of balance in the deity, as of balance in the family, that makes that creed a sort of sanity, and that sanity the soul of civilization."[22] It is crucial to Chesterton that Monophysite belief (Christ's having one nature) paved the road to Islam, which denies that God could be a man. Muhammad was in fact a Monophysite.[23] It is crucial to Chesterton that the Latin Church added to its Creed the Augustinian formulation *filioque* to describe the Holy Spirit ("through the Father *and the Son,* He is worshipped and glorified"), because the Trinity is an expression of social love that makes a cultural impact. Chesterton's rival H. G. Wells disposed of the *filioque* as "one of those impalpable and elusive doctrinal points upon which there is no reconciliation."[24] Wells was on the right side of history, it seemed, and consideration of these matters has long been dismissed by the progressive mind-set as "medieval." In the nice Orwellian upshot of such things, anti-Christian intellectuals continue to cleanse our collective memory of the Christian past. At the same time, areas of Europe are "reverting" to Islam. Forces converge, "parting sooner or later on their ways," as Pater was pleased

21. Chesterton, *Collected Works,* 1:339, 215, 88, 305.
22. G. K. Chesterton, *The Everlasting Man,* 233.
23. See, for example, Johnson, *History of Christianity,* 242–43.
24. H. G. Wells, *The Outline of History: Being a Plain History of Life and Mankind,* 637.

to observe. Future generations may be in a clearer position to judge
the contributions of Trinitarianism to the Europe of memory.

Was Chesterton's mind medieval? His medievalism operates in his
belief in the unifying force of Christendom, in his sympathy for popular superstition, in his curious mingling of real piety and worldly wisdom. His economic theory of distributivism does not fit the world we
live in—with the possible exception of Vermont.[25] But generally,
Chesterton's thinking is molded and tempered by a humanistic liberalism that engages modernity. Rejecting determinism in all its forms,
he teaches that we can make social progress by learning from history.
In *Heretics,* for example, he places the aesthetic vogue of neopaganism
against the broad expanse of western history, to observe that pagan-
ism long ago failed "in the moral world." And yet there is no "science
of history," in fact all the social sciences are "merely hopeless," because
the human mind eludes quantification.[26] Man is not the measure of
history, for he is "a growing reed." The modern historian par excellence is Hegel, whose historicizing leads to history devouring itself in
its endless appetite for historicizing (that is, to historicize historicism).
It is a steady march from Hegel to Marx to the academic theorist who
degrades the past, aglow in the purity of his ideological self-
consciousness. By contrast, Chesterton beheld the past with much the
same humane realism that distinguishes *A Tale of Two Cities* and *The
Ring and the Book.* He possessed not only historical self-awareness,
including a sense that history might end, but an imaginative capacity to understand how history is lived out in our moral choices.

Tradition for Chesterton "is the democracy of the dead." It arms the
people with "noble and healthy principles that arise" from tales and

25. See Thomas H. Naylor, "Averting Self-Destruction: A Twenty-First
Century Appraisal of Distributivism." Though I am sympathetic to it in many
respects, Chesterton's economic theory of distributivism fails to meet the global
challenges of modernity. To quote *Centesimus Annus:* "More than ever, work is
work with others and work for others: it is a matter of doing something for
someone else." For John Paul, "people work with each other, sharing in a 'community of work' which embraces ever widening circles" (John Paul II, *Centesimus
Annus,* sections 31–32). These statements, which are typical of the encyclical,
run counter to Chesterton's distributivist argument "that the one and only real
type of efficiency is the turnip-headed rustic left alone with his turnip" (G. K.
Chesterton, "On Organization and Efficiency," 49).

26. Chesterton, *Collected Works,* 1:131, 117.

myths and legends, like the "chivalrous lesson of 'Jack and the Giant Killer.'" It teaches the Christian humility of "Cinderella" and "Beauty and the Beast." It shows the moral strength of rebel, child, and underdog over giant, witch, and tyrant, who populate our day under various fashionable guises, which I leave to the reader's imagination. It is certainly not a template for reaction, since Chesterton writes, "the Jacobin has more tradition than the Jacobite."[27] The Jacobin is the modernizer.

It is therefore unlikely that Chesterton ever sympathized with Pius IX's triumphalist assertion, *"La tradizione sono io!"* (I am the tradition!).[28] I make this point because it is wrong to read Chesterton as a reactionary, condemning the modern like a building rotten from top to bottom. Chesterton lived with contradictions where modernity was concerned. He is not reducible to one camp, though critics cannot help pulling or pushing him one way or the other. For example, in his fine biography of Chesterton, Roman Catholic writer Joseph Pearce Romanizes him a little too much. He quotes Chesterton's *Autobiography,* where Chesterton remembers accompanying his father down Kensington High Street on a crowded day:

> In a flash a sort of ripple ran along the line and all these eccentrics went down on their knees on the public pavement. . . . Then I realised that a sort of little dark cab or carriage had drawn up . . . and out of it came a ghost clad in flames . . . lifting long frail fingers over the crowd in blessing. And then I looked at his face and was startled with a contrast; for his face was dead pale like ivory and very wrinkled and old . . . having in every line the ruin of great beauty.

Pearce comments, "The scarlet ghost was Cardinal Manning, a prince of the Church enshrined as an ageing Prince Charming in the memory of an ageing Chesterton writing more than fifty years after the event."[29] By connecting Manning to Prince Charming and the horse-drawn carriage, Pearce highlights the fairy-tale element in Chesterton's sensibility. Let us add, in further support of Pearce's view, that the English have a warm place in their hearts for "eccentrics." Even so,

27. Ibid., 1:251, 253.
28. Pope Pius IX, quoted in Johnson, *History of Christianity,* 394.
29. Joseph Pearce, *Wisdom and Innocence: A Life of G. K. Chesterton,* 10.

Pearce leaves out something interesting. Surely the figure of flames and ivory and ruined beauty has a shade of Satan or Mr. Kurtz about it. Manning was Pius's representative in England, and Chesterton stood outside their circle. He did not so much rally to their cause, as engage in English conversations about them. It should not be forgotten that he resisted joining the Roman Church until 1922; his friend Hilaire Belloc thought it would never happen. The passage conveys an ambivalence about Roman authority and a modern depth of perspective that should not be lost.

Chesterton's favorite example of theology in the arts is Gothic architecture. Unlike the humanists who revived antiquity, Chesterton preferred Chartres to the Parthenon. He was certainly not isolated in this preference. A. W. N. Pugin gave Gothic its second birth during the reign of George IV. A devout Roman Catholic, Pugin is one of the few English architects who rivals Christopher Wren. His central teaching, that moral principles should guide architecture, shaped the career of John Ruskin. François René de Chateaubriand, Eugène Viollet-le-Duc, and William Morris are also associated with the Gothic revival.[30] In Chesterton's eyes, Gothic affirms and defines Christian culture. For instance: "Greek heroes do not grin: but gargoyles do—because they are Christian."[31] The surprise of a grotesque joy, that piquant and abrupt incongruity, as of a bizarrely happy ending, is a uniquely Christian vision.

For Chesterton, it is the "irregular equilibrium" of Gothic that most perfectly embodies Christian ideals. He finds that Christian ethics succeeds by bringing radically competing stresses into play. Aristotle had "declared that virtue was in a balance; Christianity declared it was in a conflict: the collision of two passions apparently opposite." Christendom achieves the astonishing: humility and courage, meek saints and fierce crusaders, marriages and monasteries—all sorts of oppositions—interact so that there is no "amalgam or compromise, but both things at the top of their energy."[32] A Joan of Arc, saint and warrior, peasant and patriot, harnesses contradictions in her medieval soul, which joins more of heaven and earth than the pagan soul of the

30. For Pugin's influence on Ruskin and Morris, see Paul Johnson, *Creators: From Chaucer and Dürer to Picasso and Disney,* 136–52.
31. Chesterton, *Collected Works,* 1:307.
32. Ibid., 1:297, 296.

Phaedrus, a charioteer whose winged steeds are irreconcilably opposed in nature, the white one good, the black one bad. Through the paradoxical union of competing forces, Christianity realizes more of the soul's potential than the genius of Plato or Aristotle is able to realize.

I will devote the rest of this chapter to one of Chesterton's best novels, which keeps us on the theme of Christianity and culture. The title of *The Flying Inn* catches by association a little of the flying buttress, and this association is reinforced, so to speak, by "the wreck of an old Gothic Chapel" on the grounds of the novel's villain, Lord Ivywood.[33] Published in 1914, *The Flying Inn* is a haunting prophecy of the aftermath of empire, in particular the colonizing of old Europe by Islam. It explores the clash of civilizations in an England where English politics and art must redirect themselves toward Christianity or perish. The Turkish prophet Misysra Ammon has chosen a popular spot on the English coast to air his ingenious theories on religion and culture. Lionized by an artsy crowd, he leaves his soapbox on the beach and gains entrance into the circle of Lord Ivywood, who reverts to Islam. Why does he do so? Most conspicuously, Ivywood is redesigning his house to capture Islam's otherworldly allure. Like Shaw, he approves of Islam's prohibition of alcohol. Psychologically, he finds in Islam the means to express his Nietzschean-Shavian Superman complex. The novel's athletic hero is Patrick Dalroy, an "Irish adventurer" forced to abandon his Odyssean labors in a one-man Turkish war. Dalroy's defeat foreshadows the struggle to come at home, for Ivywood has brokered a cowardly peace, consigning some women to the harem, some workers to the dole, and some vineyards to the axe. Dalroy returns to find Ivywood ruining innkeeper Humphrey Pump, victim of a teetotaling law that robs the workers of their dignity. Seizing on a legal loophole, Dalroy and Pump (also called "Hump") take the inn on the road (hence "the flying inn"), planting the sign of "The Old Ship" in a series of picaresque adventures that thwart Ivywood's despotism. These adventures are written in a style of allegorical realism, with ideas leaping boldly into incarnate life, as for instance when Dalroy and Hump encounter—in Wordsworth's Lake District—a therapy culture of milk-drinking health fanatics. In the end, Dalroy wins back his lady love, an intuitive, Austenesque heroine named Joan Brett, and prevails in a climactic battle on English soil between Christian and Muslim.

33. G. K. Chesterton, *The Flying Inn,* 118.

The theological flavor of the novel is conveyed by one of Misysra's seaside sermons: "what we bring is the only creed that has regarded what you will call in your great words the virginity of man's reason, that has put no man higher than a prophet, and has respected the solitude of God."[34] For Chesterton, heresy is a subtle problem, with vast consequences. It takes an alert intelligence to perceive heresy, and a deeper intelligence to foresee heresy's effects. Rhetorically shrewd, Misysra knows that "the virginity of man's reason" sounds quite credible. It evokes, among other things, the Kantian notion of pure reason. What he does in practice, however, is to uproot reason from the English traditions that literally humanize it.

It would be a crude distortion to say that Misysra speaks for an ideal of reason that is purely Islamic in its origins. Meeting with the Islamic reception of Aristotle in the thirteenth century, Saint Thomas Aquinas defended a philosophy of natural reason—virginal reason, if you will—that helped usher in modern science. We are reminded that orthodoxy does not mean univocality. Aquinas himself can speak in very different tones and registers; and though Aquinas and the Latin Averroist Siger of Brabant fell out over the relation between philosophy and theology, Dante united them in his allegorical heaven. A nascent Thomist, Chesterton takes full advantage of the freedom of orthodoxy.

What Chesterton suggests through Misysra's words is a seductive charm: the way heresy seizes a part of the truth and exaggerates it. The "virginity of man's reason" can lead, as it led Siger of Brabant, to the dangerous doctrine of the "two truths": religion has its truth, science has its truth, and neither God nor man can join them. That is why Aquinas reacted strongly against Siger of Brabant (the type reappears in Francis Bacon and Stephen Jay Gould), who threatened the synthesis of faith and reason that was the great Dominican's life's work. Aquinas, moreover, had cause to fear that the heresy of double-truth would spur reactionary priests to quash the upstarts of science. On the other hand, the "virginity of man's reason" can foster scientism, the negation of values by logic and statistics. It can also foster tyranny, for virginal reason can become, in less anthropocentric terms, "reason used without root, reason in the void."[35] This rootlessness is the key to

34. Ibid., 20.
35. Chesterton, *Collected Works,* 1:230.

Misysra's theories about Islamic England. When proclaimed by a religion "that has put no man higher than a prophet, and has respected the solitude of God," the virginity of reason will either be insensitive to local traditions, or it will lord over them, redefining them through someone like Misysra, who assumes absolute authority. It will not sympathize with them. By contrast, Christianity puts one man higher than a prophet; doing so, it invests radically in human nature. More, Christianity preaches the Trinity, which denies the absolute solitude of God in favor of understanding God Himself as a society.

The threat of despotism in Misysra's theology is compounded by the strange beauty of Islamic art. As the "Prophet of the Moon" makes his way among the smart set, Chesterton observes how Islam and impressionism intersect. At issue is the increasing abstraction of modern art, its effacement of what Misysra in his comical accent calls "ze man form." This dehumanized aesthetic, soon to be remarked by real-life cultural critics like Ortega y Gasset, prepares the way for the superhuman designs of Ivywood, who senses his own sublime vocation in the shimmering arabesques and melting distances of the East; at the same time, the effacement of man from western art parallels the indifference, on the part of England's ruling elite, to the people's real interests.

The Flying Inn is a minor masterpiece of Christian humanism. Its comic conceit is our unconsciousness before the perils that threaten our civilization. Chesterton warns that the fashions of art are never theologically neutral, though they may be naive. He shows a fine Swiftian appreciation for scheming politicians and conceited authors. Granted, he is not deeply refined in handling character, but he is in moral revolt against excessive psychologizing. He maintains a vivid sense of the mystery of others, despite his stubborn preference for realism over impressionism. If you compare the orators on the beach in *The Flying Inn* to the orators in Hyde Park in Woolf's *The Years,* you will find the former are more alive. Chesterton takes from Dickens an element of caricature that attacks our perception with a robust shock. Most important, his protagonists retain a physical wholeness of viewpoint that is increasingly rare. It is only the whole man who knows what ails the aesthetes, the therapists, and the governing class.

3

T. S. ELIOT (1888–1965)

From Delmore Schwartz to James E. Miller Jr., Eliot's personal life has inspired morbid fascination. Though Dr. Johnson teaches us to notice the intersections of art and character, yet the light shed on Eliot's private experience is almost invariably sallow. He and Vivienne Haigh-Wood suffered through an ill-fated marriage, which terminated in misery for both parties. Late in life, he made a happy second marriage to his secretary, Valerie Fletcher, forty years his junior. He may have been a virgin; he may have been bisexual, or maybe he wasn't homosexual at all. There is no first-rate biography, and certainly none has done justice to Eliot's underlying courage. Eliot was a skilled and daring sailor, despite a congenital double hernia that kept him from serving in the U.S. Navy. He gave up a safe career teaching philosophy, and defied his wealthy father, by settling in a foreign country to make his own way. He was a London fire warden during World War II, watching from the roof of his office building, in Russell Square, as the Luftwaffe dropped bombs on the darkened city. There is a heroic vigilance behind the delicate moods of the poetry. The central story of Eliot's life, his journey from Unitarian unbelief to Christian faith in the shadow of modern skepticism, illuminates his writings and ranks among the great conversion stories in the arts.

Eliot arrived in London in August 1914, about three weeks after Germany declared war on Russia. He found the city "foreign, but hospitable, or rather tolerant." A born anthropologist, he made a close study of English society and soon adjusted to life in London and Oxford. Being American, he invented himself as he went along. He was a philosopher, a mystic, a poet, a critic, and a banker. He taught literature to lower-class men and upper-class boys. By all accounts, he was refined: "Eliot was never once (except on holiday) photographed without a tie, wore three piece suits on all occasions, and was the last intellectual on either side of the Atlantic to wear spats." He talked and dressed with "the Puritan refinement of Boston" that amused Chesterton when he met his new neighbor, the novelist Henry James.[1]

By 1920, when he published *The Sacred Wood,* Eliot had established himself as one of the leading innovators on the literary scene. His modernist writing was an aggressive form of aestheticism, which did not retreat from society but challenged it. He began *The Sacred Wood* by distinguishing the critic of literature from the critic at large. "Some persons," he writes, "like Mr. Wells and Mr. Chesterton, have succeeded so well in . . . setting the house in order, . . . that we must conclude that it is indeed their proper role, and that they have done well for themselves in laying literature aside."[2] *The Sacred Wood* was certainly a reinvestment in literary authority, but it was something more, a work rife with implications for a revolutionary social order disciplined by art. Its author was a sophisticated type of aesthetic humanist, who deferred to neither nature nor reason, but made them do his bidding. Wilde had already established that "Life imitates Art far more than Art imitates Life," and "external nature also imitates Art." In the age of cubism and jazz, nature would have some additional catching up to do. The highest creative goal was, Eliot said, "to state a vision."[3] Whether the vision came from Aquinas or Lobachevsky, reason would cooperate.

We have seen that Chesterton distrusted the aesthetic movement. He says of the aesthetic type: "The artistic temperament is a disease that afflicts amateurs. It is a disease which arises from men not having sufficient power of expression to utter and get rid of the element of art in their being." Trickily, Eliot agreed. He applied much the same argument to the poet-critic Arthur Symons, whom he rightly called "the critical successor of Pater" (Pater had numerous successors, including Wilde and Yeats): "The disturbance in Mr. Symons is almost, but not quite, to the point of creating; . . . but it is not the expulsion,

---

1. T. S. Eliot, *The Letters of T. S. Eliot, 1898–1922,* 1:55; Johnson, *Creators,* 204; Chesterton, *Collected Works,* 16:210.
2. T. S. Eliot, *The Sacred Wood: Essays on Poetry and Criticism,* xiii–xiv.
3. Oscar Wilde, *Complete Works of Oscar Wilde,* 992; Eliot, *Sacred Wood,* 170.

the ejection, the birth of creativeness." "The type is not uncommon," adds Eliot, "although Mr. Symons is far superior to most of the type."[4] Eliot himself was able to create true poetry. He is one of the glories of our language. What then is the essential difference that separates his view of art from Chesterton's?

Let us turn for a moment to that Rorschach test of the artistic personality: Shakespeare. Chesterton's bard is a Renaissance man, not at all a modern specialist: "Shakespeare had a real lyrical impulse, wrote a real lyric, and so got rid of the impulse and went about his business. Being an artist did not prevent him from being an ordinary man, any more than being a sleeper at night or being a diner at dinner prevented him from being an ordinary man." Chesterton hated artistic pretension and delighted in correcting it: "There can be no stronger manifestation of the man who is a really great artist than the fact that he can dismiss the subject of art; that he can, on due occasion, wish art to the bottom of the sea." Like Prospero, then, Chesterton's Shakespeare has a perspective that transcends his art.[5]

Eliot's Shakespeare is a tortured intellectual. In *Hamlet,* we are told, "he attempted to express the inexpressibly horrible." Here we cannot fail to recognize the author of *The Waste Land.* Eliot's artistic preoccupations are, in his sense, Shakespearean, reflecting a tortuous approach to the meaning of his "personal experience." In "The Metaphysical Poets," Eliot describes a "telescoping of images and multiplied associations" that is "characteristic" of Shakespeare and Donne. He then asserts the contemporary relevance of metaphysical poetry: "Our civilization comprehends great variety and complexity, and this variety and complexity, playing upon a refined sensibility, must produce various and complex results. The poet must become more and more comprehensive, more allusive, more indirect, in order to force, to dislocate if necessary, language into his meaning." This passage, which shows the modernist aesthetic at its most ambitious, derives from Pater's critique of habit: "In a sense it might even be said that our failure is to

---

4. Chesterton, *Collected Works,* 1:171; Eliot, *Sacred Wood,* 2–3, 6. Chesterton's passage echoes Pater: "Few artists . . . work quite cleanly, casting off all *débris,* and leaving us only what the heat of their imagination has wholly fused and transformed" (Pater, *Works,* 1:x–xi).

5. Chesterton, *Collected Works,* 1:173, 172. "And deeper than did ever plummet sound / I'll drown my book" (*The Tempest* 5.1.56–57).

form habits: for, after all, habit is relative to a stereotyped world, and meantime it is only the roughness of the eye that makes any two persons, things, situations, seem alike."[6] But compared to Pater, or even to Shakespeare, Eliot is doing something harder: he is trying to reorder language, to change the associative patterns of speech, and, by implication, society itself. His poems (despite his theorizing) can be quite personal, but their authority resides in their being perfect aesthetic objects or pure works of art. His images and symbols refer constantly to their own transcendent idea, that is, to the poetic faith behind them.

And so there is a powerful contrast. Chesterton is comical, democratic, and orthodox. Eliot is ironic, aristocratic, and a priest of art. Chesterton shows a Lincolnesque loyalty to the people, Eliot stands aloof from the cliché-ridden mass mind.[7] Chesterton's *Orthodoxy* is a work of understanding seeking faith; Eliot's *Waste Land* is a work of faith seeking understanding. Chesterton despises the fact-value dichotomy, Eliot hails the authority of technical science. Chesterton's tradition is a "democracy of the dead," Eliot's is an "ideal order of existing monuments." Chesterton sees a wall between East and West, and Eliot in *The Waste Land* transcends it.

The London that Eliot mapped and mastered was rapidly modernizing, despite economic hardship. So strong were the differences between the young veterans and the Georgian establishment that London became, in effect, two cities. *Gerontion,* which means "little old man," comments on the moral failure of the old guard, who "neither fought at the hot gates / nor fought in the warm rain." In this dramatic monologue, Eliot conveys a message that Chesterton, with his medieval roots, refused to countenance. It was more than a picture of spiritual division. It was a vision of the Void. Among the disillusioned young artists, the values and insights of Chesterton seemed stale, dead and useless. Western civilization was "botched," in Pound's words, "an old bitch gone in the teeth."[8]

A cultural breakthrough was desperately needed, and philosophers and artists labored furiously to produce one. There was a tremendous

---

6. Eliot, *Selected Essays,* 126, 243, 248; Pater, *Works,* 1:236–37.

7. For this contrast, see John Carey, *The Intellectuals and the Masses: Pride and Prejudice among the Literary Intelligensia, 1880–1939.*

8. T. S. Eliot, *Collected Poems, 1909–1962,* 29; Ezra Pound, *Personae,* 191.

amount of data coming out of the sciences, the impact of which Chesterton underestimated. Scientists were looking at reality in ways that had little to do with the workaday world; few middle-class people could follow the new physics, which was running away like the dish with the spoon. In 1919 Eliot announced his new synthesis in "Tradition and the Individual Talent," which became the centerpiece of *The Sacred Wood.* Many years later, he remarked that his "earliest critical essays . . . came to seem to me the product of immaturity." He referred to his most famous essay as "juvenile," although he "did not repudiate" it.[9] The improvisatory genius of his early criticism does at times lend itself to illusory gains. Eliot shuns the burden of metaphysics. Instead, he proceeds by a series of small victories that do not necessarily add up to a convincing whole. His central strategy is to turn our attention to ideal constructions of the real. In effect, he occupies a borderland between fiction and reality. He describes art as an autonomous realm, an independent aesthetic structure, known to the mind. While discarding ultimate reality and denaturing art, he dazzles with metaphors from science and philosophy. As always, his taste is exquisite.

Eliot's "Impersonal theory" of art keeps life at a distance. It is a Cartesian theory, which detaches pure mind from the body's machinery.[10] Emotion gives way to "art emotion," and mimesis gives way to abstraction. For Eliot, "the difference between art and event is always absolute."[11] This part of his theory runs fully counter to Aristotle's *Poetics,* and it is a marvel of aesthetic engineering that Eliot can cite Aristotle continually throughout *The Sacred Wood,* since the difference between art and event is not absolute to the physical man pierced by the tragic emotion of catharsis. For Aristotle, it is the emotions of the body that mediate between life and art.

After he was received into the Church of England in 1927, Eliot was able to connect his modernist aesthetic to Augustinian theology. He had already paid homage to Saint Augustine by alluding to him in *The Waste Land* as an exemplar of "western asceticism." More, the

---

9. Eliot, "Preface to the Edition of 1964," in Eliot, *Use of Poetry,* n.p.

10. Though he rejects Descartes, Eliot displays Cartesian tendencies despite himself. See my *Ethics of Modernism: Moral Ideas in Yeats, Eliot, Joyce, Woolf, and Beckett,* 2–3, 51–52, 63–64, 134n9.

11. Eliot, *Sacred Wood,* 56.

link between aesthetics and theology had suggested itself in numerous earlier poems. Among the most prominent of these is *Gerontion,* where the old man's reverie expresses the religious crisis of Europe. The abyssal Eucharist of lines 19–29 features a cast of spiritual aliens, Hakagawa, Madame de Tornquist, and Fräulein von Kulp, whose enigmatic actions reflect a cosmopolitan society in anomic decay. Their lives inspire a devastating anagnorisis, in the verse paragraph beginning, "After such knowledge, what forgiveness? Think now."[12]

Eliot formally *enacts* the fall of man by placing the imperatives "Think now" (lines 33 and 36) and "Think" (line 43) at the ends of lines at cascading intervals. Through personification, an image emerges of history as the Whore of Babylon, vitiating "our" will. Her fatal attractions allow "us" no earthly escape. For Augustine and Eliot, skepticism about human powers reinforces a tendency toward asceticism, isolating the soul on its journey—toward God or the Void. Being "unable to speak" the word or inner truth of God, humanity fails as first, the virtues, and then, the senses, break down: "I have lost my sight, smell, hearing, taste and touch: / How should I use them for your closer contact?"[13] The helpless soul can only watch the body's fate with horror.

The first book of cultural criticism from the Christian Eliot is *After Strange Gods: A Primer of Modern Heresy,* based on his lectures at the University of Virginia in 1933. I am inclined to believe that Eliot took the scheme of orthodoxy and heresy from Chesterton. It may be replied that the terms have wide currency. There is, for instance, the witty remark by Bishop Warburton: "Orthodoxy is my doxy; heterodoxy is another man's doxy." But Eliot, who would have appreciated that little sally, in fact mentions Chesterton's economic theory of distributivism as an influence on his own work, and the branding of living authors as heretics has, to the best of my knowledge, no other precedent in recent criticism.

Only a dozen or so years after the aesthetic retrenchment of *The Sacred Wood,* Eliot was entering on Chesterton's territory. But Eliot was more doubtful of modern western democracy than Chesterton was. Chesterton, after all, called himself a liberal, while Eliot held liberalism in contempt.

---

12. Eliot, *Collected Poems,* 30.
13. Ibid., 31.

We have considered the basic differences between the two thinkers; here we might especially notice the quietism of Eliot's first Christian poems. In *Ash-Wednesday,* Eliot followed his theology to its logical conclusion and preached grace without works: "Teach us to care and not to care, / Teach us to sit still."[14] If there was one thing that Chesterton could not do, it was that.

After Strange Gods is morally puzzling because its author, a world-famous artist, does not address the relation between aesthetics and ethics, the beautiful and the good, Athens and Jerusalem. Eliot writes in his preface: "I ascended the platform of these lectures only in the role of a moralist."[15] Declining to discuss the art of literature, he proceeds to issue a scathing indictment of modernist writers on moral grounds. Arnold, let us be fair, had something to offer in his synthesis of Hebraism and Hellenism, only he stumbled badly in thinking that the poet could assume the mantle of the priest. Chesterton had no tolerance for novels whose clear literary superiority entailed a snobby and vicious outlook on life. For Chesterton, literature was finally not that important. But Eliot the moralist and Eliot the artist could not even hold a conversation.

The Virginia lectures show a great mind exhausted by its own divisions. The brilliant modernist, hounded by guilt and self-doubt, expresses his moral revulsion at modernism. Eliot's ostensible purpose is to revise his notion of literary tradition to fit with his Christianity. But what we are forced to witness is Eliot's injury and mutilation (strong word) as a defender of orthodoxy: "a *tradition* is rather a way of feeling and acting which characterises a group throughout generations; . . . it must largely be . . . unconscious; whereas the maintenance of *orthodoxy* is a matter which calls for the exercise of all our conscious intelligence." The lectures' most notorious comment is an exercise of orthodox judgment that would safeguard tradition: "reasons of race and religion combine to make any large number of free-thinking Jews undesirable" in an agrarian community of the type that Eliot specifically has in mind.[16] It is the "race," not the "religion" side of the argument that is repugnant; a genuine pluralism, after all, is not the same as multicultural conformity. Reliving the Dreyfus case in Virginia, Eliot blames free-thinking Jews for the

14. Ibid., 95. I am indebted to R. W. B. Lewis, *Dante,* 176.
15. T. S. Eliot, *After Strange Gods,* 10.
16. Ibid., 31, 20.

absence of a living tradition (he would prefer less intellectual strain—he detests modernity and the conscious adjustment of art and morals), and he blames Mansfield, Lawrence, Pound, and Yeats for sins he has himself committed. Protesting too much, he begins to look, on the artistic side, remarkably like a modernist free-thinking Jew.[17] Along with Chesterton, he believed that "unity of religious background" protected tradition.[18] This is an important point, and it should not be ruled out of bounds by critics of religious conservatism. But the problems with Eliot's own effort at cultural synthesis go beyond the tension between Jew and Christian and have nothing to do with race. Eliot was transfixed by the tragic flaw in western culture: the stubborn breach between orthodoxy and tradition, between thought and feeling, between sensibility and conscience. He was staring paralytically at the wide, wide distance between Athens and Jerusalem; for so confounding is that distance, so crippling the contradictions inhabiting it, that the heroic Chesterton may be wrong—in which case no wondrous balance, no gothic miracle of thought and feeling, can grace our civilization.

As the foundations of Europe seemed to disintegrate, the aesthetes packed their wardrobes in a kind of flight. They abandoned the rational, naturalistic Athens of Matthew Arnold, and populated the decadent, beautiful Athens of Walter Pater. But Eliot led the modernists in the oddest turn of all. He renamed his city of art Jerusalem:

> What is that sound high in the air
> Murmur of maternal lamentation
> Who are those hooded hordes swarming
> Over endless plains, stumbling in cracked earth
> Ringed by the flat horizon only
> What is the city over the mountains
> Cracks and reforms and bursts in the violet air
> Falling towers
> Jerusalem Athens Alexandria
> Vienna London
> Unreal[19]

17. On this topic, see William Empson, *Using Biography,* 189–200.
18. Eliot, *After Strange Gods,* 20.
19. Eliot, *Collected Poems,* 67.

This stunning panorama has moral qualities but no moral substance. Certainly, the exacting technique and style of *The Waste Land* have moral qualities. But Eliot's conjunction of morality and aesthetics is an ethereal vision. At this revelatory height, East meets West, history hangs by a thread, and we swim in the "unreal" maya. But what is the truth of this dolorous beauty? Is God or fate behind it? Where does it tend? If we speak of compassion, we need to ask, on what grounds are we to be compassionate? Do reason and free will enter the vision? Throughout his major works, Eliot escapes his own sense of moral failure through mysticism. As I have suggested, *The Waste Land* is a work of mystical faith seeking understanding: that is what it *means,* and that is how its mythical wilderness comes to life.

Eliot labors under the quintessential modernist difficulty of moral solitude, and that is why he ascends such a stilted platform in Virginia. He proposes a mind-body dualism for the consciously orthodox and the unconsciously traditional. The orthodox mind is cut off from the world it surveys. It can shift perspective, but it cannot shift its weight, since it has none. Likewise, "the mind of Europe" can compose *The Waste Land,* and the same mind can envision the green valley of Christian agrarianism. But Eliot suffers from a Cartesian debility, or Augustinian distrust of the body, that prevents him from bringing the good and the beautiful into the harmony of noble action, or from supporting modern democratic culture as an expression of such actions. He is thoroughly doubtful of the ethics of democracy.

The case for a democratic turn in the later Eliot rests on a series of lectures that he gave in 1950 at the University of Chicago called "The Aims of Education."[20] The lectures focus on two concerns of Eliot's, democracy and education, that he usually approaches through religion. For instance, Eliot writes in a 1933 lecture, "Modern Education and the Classics": "to know what we want in education we must know what we want in general, we must derive our theory of education from our philosophy of life. The problem turns out to be a religious problem."[21] And in *The Idea of a Christian Society,* from 1939, he responds to historian Christopher Dawson's warnings about "totalitarian democracy": "To those who can imagine . . . such a prospect, one can assert that the only possibility of control and balance is a religious control and bal-

20. Jeffrey Perl makes the case in *Skepticism and Modern Enmity,* 119–20.
21. T. S. Eliot, *Essays Ancient and Modern,* 169.

ance; that the only hopeful course for a society which would thrive
and continue its creative activity in the arts of civilisation, is to become
Christian."[22] By not immediately erecting his religious framework in
"The Aims of Education," Eliot appears to be more cordially disposed
to modern western democracies and their educational agendas than
previously. He applies his background in Bradleyan idealism to a non-
religious analysis of the key words *democracy* and *education*. He easily
demonstrates that the meaning of these words changes according to
one's point of view, and that no single definition can suffice to illuminate the network of meanings and associations that follows these big
abstractions on their daily rounds.

Eliot was always doubtful of the Arnoldian vision of middle-class
liberal education, but his doubts deepened and matured as Stalin and
Hitler rose to power. They distorted the political landscape beyond
reckoning, and if time has not rectified the ideological confusion that
burst the dam of sense with the Nazi-Soviet Nonaggression Pact, it
has not superannuated Eliot's worries about democratic education.
These were basically consistent throughout his career as a Christian
cultural critic. It is a small step from the conservative, class-based politics of *Notes towards the Definition of Culture,* from 1948, to the apparently more democratic outlook of "The Aims of Education," where
Eliot responds to critics of the earlier book more by elaboration than
by revision. Though he is "not denying that democracy is the best
form of society" *(Notes),* and though "we all agree on the affirmation
that a democracy is the best possible aim for society" ("Aims"),[23] neither statement is conclusive, because the meaning of democracy is
inherently protean and unstable. The rabbit that Eliot pulls out of
his wopsical hat in Chicago is that he cannot answer the problem of
education in a modern western democracy; all he can do is improve
our understanding of the problem. He is not dramatically inspiring;

22. T. S. Eliot, *The Idea of a Christian Society,* 19. He defines "totalitarian
democracy" as "a state of affairs in which we shall have regimentation and conformity, without respect for the needs of the individual soul; the puritanism of
hygienic morality in the interest of efficiency; uniformity of opinion through
propaganda, and art encouraged only when it flatters the official doctrines of
the time" (ibid., 18).

23. T. S. Eliot, *Notes towards the Definition of Culture,* 175; T. S. Eliot, *To Criticize
the Critic and Other Writings,* 70.

he is calmly terrifying. His lectures are written from a height that dwarfs liberal and conservative, and that casts the whole enterprise of secular education in doubt.

Both in *Notes towards the Definition of Culture* and in "The Aims of Education," Eliot takes issue with the anti-Christian writer C. E. M. Joad, an educator who became famous in England through the BBC radio show *Brains Trust,* and whom Eliot identifies with Chesterton's old adversaries, Wells and Shaw.[24] The center of the debate is Joad's three ends of education:

> To enable a boy or girl to make his or her living.
> To equip him to play his part as a citizen in a democracy.
> To enable him to develop all the latent powers and faculties of his nature and so enjoy a good life.[25]

"The ideal," Eliot comments, "is a life in which one's livelihood, one's functions as a citizen, and one's self-development all fit into and enhance each other." This ideal life is threatened because democracy oscillates in practice between libertarianism and authoritarianism, with the latter the likely winner in a power struggle. The only real bulwark against democratic tyranny is (it turns out after all) the Church, which can nourish the community: "The religious sense, and the sense of community, cannot be finally divorced from each other."[26]

To get his point across, Eliot observes the machinery of what Barzun calls "the Great Switch," "the reversal of liberalism into its opposite."[27] Barzun traces the phenomenon in England to the writings of Shaw and the government of Lloyd George. Looming above these historical particulars, Eliot applies the abstract rhetoric of sociology. Religion, he writes impersonally,

> ceases to inform the whole of life; then a vacuum is discovered, and the belief in religion will be gradually supplanted by a belief in the

---

24. Joad converted to Anglicanism at the end of his life, publishing *The Recovery of Belief* in 1952. See Joseph Pearce, *Literary Converts: Spiritual Inspiration in an Age of Unbelief,* 277–78.

25. Eliot, *To Criticize the Critic,* 69.

26. Ibid., 103, 113.

27. Barzun, *From Dawn to Decadence,* 688.

State. That part of the social life which is independent of the State will be diminished to the more trivial. The necessity will appear for a common belief in *something* to fill the place of religion in the community; and the liberals will find themselves surrendering more and more of the individual freedom which was the basis of their doctrine.[28]

Eliot cites equal opportunity as an example of educational policy that "might tend to limit education to the kinds of training which served the immediate purposes of the State."[29] The problem is that once the "purposes of the State" begin to shape education, they inevitably grow in scope and importance. And if government is given universal and exclusive control over who is educated and how, there is just no guarantee that democratic citizenship will contribute to anybody's happiness. A rotten democracy will frustrate its own people by dictating the terms of good and bad citizenship, much as the czars of diversity fleece and frustrate students of all social backgrounds.

So the most important of the three needs of education turns out to be the last, which leads reflective persons to a further set of questions, "What is the good life?" "What is Man?" Although Eliot relies considerably on the light of reason to open his religious perspective, it is faith that supplies the answers and orients us in our professions, our citizenship, and our lives: "It is the province of our religious teachers to instruct us in our latent powers and tell us which are good and which are bad, and to give a definite meaning to the improvement of 'man as man.'"[30] But we are hardly home free. Eliot's sense of Original Sin tinctures his speculations on the human potential for happiness to the point of twilight. He cites the words of Simone Weil and her disciple Gustave Thibon—words revealing a deeply rooted unhappiness at the heart of civilization:

> The soul devoted to the pursuit of the absolutely good meets in this world with insoluble contradictions. "Our life is impossibility, absurdity. Everything that we will is contradicted by the conditions or by the consequences attached to it. That is because we are ourselves contradiction, being merely creatures . . ." If, for example,

28. Eliot, *To Criticize the Critic,* 114.
29. Ibid., 103.
30. Ibid., 113.

you have innumerable children: that tends to bring about overpopulation and war (the typical case in Japan). If you improve the material conditions of the people: you risk spiritual deterioration. If you devote yourself utterly to some person—you cease to exist for that person. Only imaginary goods imply no contradiction: the girl who desires a large family, the social reformer who dreams of the happiness of the people—such individuals do not encounter any obstacle so long as they refrain from action. They sail along happily in a good which is absolute, but fictitious: to stumble against reality is the signal for waking up. This contradiction, the mark of our wretchedness and our greatness, is something that we must accept in all its bitterness.[31]

It is unsurprising that the author of *Gerontion* was drawn to this debunking of progressive consolations. For Weil, an Augustinian acceptance of hardship and suffering serves to concentrate our spiritual attention. The Thomistic effort to reconcile Aristotelian ethics and biblical theology is tragically voided. Given the overwhelming difficulties that Thibon describes, it is hard to say what the aim of education could possibly be in the City of Man. The fact that Eliot consistently defends what Arnold called "knowledge of the best that has been thought and said in the world," especially the Greek and Latin classics, confirms, in effect, that Eliot envisions education such that only "a small number of people can be educated well."[32] He is certainly not espousing Arnoldian liberal humanism for the middle class.

To read Eliot sympathetically is to bear in mind the potentially fruitful tension, which he explores, between high classical culture and modern democratic culture, between aristocratic ideals and the best goals of Christian education.[33] He wants to keep "the achievement principle" alive and to avoid conformity and regimentation. Humanism survives as "a mediating and corrective ingredient in a positive civilization founded on definite belief." It is never a creed, never a substitute for a

31. Ibid., 91–92. Weil's words are in quotation marks. The ellipses are either Thibon's or Eliot's.

32. Ibid., 119–20.

33. See the second chapter of *Notes towards the Definition of Culture*, 107–22, as well as the 1946 lecture "The Unity of Culture," ibid., 187–202. See also the highly relevant note by Werner Jaeger, *Paideia: The Ideals of Greek Culture*, 417n6.

creed. It occupies a mediatory role between social classes, between regions, and between nations. It enriches Christian culture with a capacity to assimilate rival ideas. All that humanism "can ask, in the most tolerant spirit, is: Is this particular philosophy or religion civilized or is it not?"[34] Maybe that is not so little after all.

By contrast, the "New Humanism" of Irving Babbitt looked to Eliot like another form of heretical spirituality. Eliot was especially rattled by *Democracy and Leadership,* a book where his former teacher rejected Christianity and offered in its place the elite satisfactions of moral intuitionism, which Babbitt hoped would save American civilization. "It is Humanism's positivistic tendencies that are alarming," Eliot commented in 1929. "In the work of the master, and still more in that of the disciples, there is a tendency towards a positive and exclusive dogma. Conceive a Comtism from which all the absurdities had been removed . . . and you have something like what I imagine humanism might become."[35] In *After Strange Gods,* Eliot went on to explain Babbitt in terms of agnosticism and "the decay of Protestantism."[36] The younger Eliot was Babbitt's protegé, sharing his "positivistic tendencies" and post-Protestant culture. But given Eliot's Christian premises, the New Humanism could do nothing to direct humanity to the good life.[37] It could, however, contribute to totalitarian democracy by neutralizing the Church. Or just as frightening, it could spur its disillusioned followers into a distorted reaction: "a Catholicism *without* the element of humanism and criticism, which would be a Catholicism of despair."[38]

Far removed from the battles of his youth, Eliot does not attack the particular democratic bias of his audience in Chicago, but he drops hints that he cannot reach them. He suggests why his undertaking is (in his own words) "a wild-goose chase": "In my 'aims of education' it is not the place of religion in education, but the place of education in

34. Eliot, *Selected Essays,* 436.
35. Ibid., 430 (dated in *Selected Essays* as 1928). I follow Gallup's date of 1929; see Donald Gallup, *T. S. Eliot: A Bibliography,* 223.
36. Eliot, *After Strange Gods,* 41.
37. Chesterton's response to the New Humanism is close to Eliot's in the essentials. See Chesterton's 1929 essay, "Is Humanism a Religion?" in *The Thing: Why I Am a Catholic,* in *Collected Works,* 3:146–56.
38. Eliot, *Selected Essays,* 426.

religion, that is the vital issue."[39] A rhetorical chiasmus (from the Greek letter χ, or *chi*) normally creates an inversion of terms that lends itself to oxymoron and pun. My sense here is that Eliot, in a sublime formal pun, is crossing out the terms of his argument, and gesturing at their futility. His real point is that we have missed the point: education ceases to occur once religion has been expelled from the public square, since real education is ordered toward the good of man by religion. Eliot is, I suggest, a theocrat, though he wants a humanistic theocracy that maximizes freedom in accordance with his own somber worldview. Further, in light of his sensitivity to political language, we ought to recognize that *theocracy* is a word with a wide range of meanings. For example, Rémi Brague argues: "Whether the underlying idea of democracy is law or conscience, . . . both ideas have theological underpinnings. Hence, our democratic ideals both of a rule of law and of a moral awareness that is expected to serve as a final authority in the mind and soul of every human being are theologically grounded."[40] In this respect, a radically nontheocratic regime may not be democratically possible.

Though he camouflages himself with a sociological idiom that sounds perfectly, almost devoutly, modern, Eliot arrives at the same point as Chesterton: it is religion that makes the best life possible for man. But with Eliot's Augustinian modernism, we lose Chesterton's dynamic hopefulness. The author of *Orthodoxy* became a champion of Saint Thomas Aquinas, whose life and work he described in a book that helped popularize neo-Thomism. Published in 1933, *Saint Thomas Aquinas: The Dumb Ox* concludes with an attack on the Augustinian theology of Luther, the preface to a modernity that Eliot turned to his creative advantage, almost despite himself. But 1922 was the year

---

39. Eliot, *To Criticize the Critic,* 116.

40. Rémi Brague, "Are Non-Theocratic Regimes Possible?" 6. In a paper on Eliot and Christopher Dawson, Benjamin Lockerd shows persuasively that Eliot, like Dawson, rejected any "sort of medieval theocratic government." Lockerd cites two passages from *The Idea of a Christian Society:* "We know from our reading of history, that a certain tension between Church and State is desirable." And "it must be kept in mind that even in a Christian society as well organised as we can conceive possible in this world, the limit would be that our temporal and spiritual life should be harmonised: the temporal and the spiritual would never be identified" (Eliot, *Idea of a Christian Society,* 71, 44).

when Chesterton lost the artistic battle. It was the year of *The Waste Land* and *Ulysses*. It was also the year of Chesterton's conversion to Rome, a turning that was also a turning away, a triumph with a haunting element of loss. As modernism won the day—one thinks of Evelyn Waugh's description of Oxford in the 1920s, in *Brideshead Revisited*—Chesterton's romance of history seemed to fail.

4

J. R. R. Tolkien (1892–1973)

Of the three major writers at the center of this book, Tolkien's climb to fame was by far the steepest. His father died when he was three and his brother just a toddler. His diabetic mother was ostracized because of her conversion to Rome. She died when he was twelve. Thereafter, a parish priest looked after the boys. Tolkien fought in the trenches of World War I, which decimated his circle of friends. While in uniform he married a fellow orphan named Edith Bratt. The young couple saw their fortunes begin to rise when he passed his entrance exam for Oxford University, where he would eventually teach. As one of the world's authorities on Old and Middle English, he worked with many talented students, including W. H. Auden, whose Anglo-Saxon landscapes renewed the English lyric in the 1930s, and who became a friend and ally. Ronald and Edith had three boys and one girl. It was a loving family, despite some strains between husband and wife.

With regard to the supercilious contempt that has long been directed at Middle-earth, it can truly be said that never have so many critics done so little with so much. I will not lavish time on the crowings; others have discussed them judiciously and *in extenso*.[1] But it will be helpful to explore the differences in sensibility that divide Tolkien from the modernists, especially since Tolkien fell afoul of the modernist aesthetic that Eliot represented.

I go back to Pater's obsession with style, which has its inspiration (Pater tells us) in Flaubert. By sacrificing personal happiness for sty-

---

1. See Joseph Pearce, *Tolkien: Man and Myth;* and Bradley J. Birzer, *J. R. R. Tolkien's Sanctifying Myth: Understanding Middle-earth.*

listic perfection, Flaubert embraced artistic martyrdom. The Flaubertian author is impersonal and godlike, detached from popular sentiment, and much given to scrupulous observation. He regards justice as an aesthetic discipline *(le mot juste)*, a flawless surface, not a virtue arising from the depths of human nature or the wisdom of God. Flaubert is skeptical about human relations, especially love and marriage. He invites us to study the world as he sees it, with a cold eye. He is unmoved by our emotional needs.

In all this, Flaubert lays the groundwork for modernism. Pater and Eliot follow him by aestheticizing conscience through the medium of style, where a cliché betrays a lack of artistic virtue. Even in *Four Quartets,* Eliot inherits from the aesthetic movement a mental reflex against convention. When he accuses himself of a lapse, it is not a sin or a vice in the ordinary sense. It is a "periphrastic study in a worn-out poetical fashion."[2] The failure is artistic: the spirit is caged in a dead style.

In contrast to Flaubert's aestheticism, Tolkien puts the story first and the style second. Arnold defended this type of approach in his 1853 preface, which centers on the "cultivated Athenian" who "required that the permanent elements of his nature should be moved." Likewise, Tolkien describes the "prime motive" behind *The Lord of the Rings* as "the desire of a tale-teller to try his hand at a really long story that would hold the attention of readers, amuse them, delight them, and at times maybe excite them or deeply move them." Tolkien aims for what Arnold called "unity and profoundness of moral impression."[3] The reader is assumed to identify emotionally with the protagonist. Vice and virtue are more than "materials for art."[4] The reign of style over story is not just a revolution in taste: it is a watershed in the history of art. The modernist is no friend to human nature; typically, he wants to transform it through the use of art. The tale-teller embraces human nature, sings to the heart, and humanizes the soul.

For the tale-teller, style has its place, which is subordinate to "the spirit of the whole."[5] The William Morris coloring of Lothlórien is,

2. Eliot, *Collected Poems,* 184.

3. Arnold, *Complete Prose Works,* 1:6; J. R. R. Tolkien, foreword to *The Fellowship of the Ring,* 6; Arnold, *Complete Prose Works,* 1:12.

4. "Vice and virtue are to the artist materials for an art" (Wilde, *Complete Works,* 17).

5. Arnold, *Complete Prose Works,* 1:9.

by modernist standards, hackneyed and trite: "At the feet of the trees, and all about the green hillsides the grass was studded with small golden flowers shaped like stars. Among them, nodding on slender stalks, were other flowers, white and palest green: they glimmered as a mist amidst the rich hue of the grass." The expert modernist will be able to date and analyze the style, in accordance with Pound's famous dictum, "Make it new." Elizabeth Bishop, for instance, is able to redeem the likes of "palest green" by updating her idiom, describing a planet in a conversational tone as "the pale green one."[6] By comparison, the tale-teller will look on the modernist as a fragmented being who cannot see the forest for the trees: the modernist has lost all sense of proportion and neglects the great unfolding of the tale.

A masterful plot is among the most exhilarating experiences in art. When a story line catches fire, we respond viscerally, physically in the beating of the rib cage and the tingling of the spine. To hold that there is a relation between art and life is not to hold that art and life are the same: that is just a way of exalting art for art's sake. It is a civilized pleasure to survey the drama of life, to be remote from real pain while participating in rich emotion and strange experience. Rarely in literature is this excitement felt as fully as in the tenth chapter of the first book of *The Lord of the Rings,* the chapter called "Strider." It is literally the chapter where Tolkien hits his stride. Until that chapter, there have been a fine prettiness, a curious tone, "Dark Riders," and picaresque adventures. But here dawns that horizon where the *Poetics* of Aristotle touches the Gospel of Mark: "a scene in which recognition of the hero" (here the mutual recognition of heroes, especially Aragorn and Frodo) "results in the friendship of those destined for good fortune and the enmity of those destined for ill."[7] When Aragorn makes himself known to the hobbits amid the hubbub of Bree and the smoke of the Prancing Pony, the story leaps into the reader's heart, presuming he has one. For the first time since *The Hobbit,* the potential of Middle-earth hits home.

Tolkien's monumental lecture "On Fairy-Stories" (1938) stands or falls by the *Poetics,* a work whose author can fairly be referred to as the founder of the tale-telling camp. Aristotle holds that "the first essen-

---

6. Tolkien, *Fellowship of the Ring,* 365; Elizabeth Bishop, *The Complete Poems, 1927–1979,* 103.
    7. Robert M. Grant, *A Historical Introduction to the New Testament,* 125.

tial, the life and soul, so to speak, of Tragedy is the Plot." "Tragedy," Tolkien writes in an Aristotelian spirit, "is the true form of the Drama, its highest function." Fairy stories accept the tragic burden of "sorrow and failure," but at their best, fairy stories have something else: "the good catastrophe, the sudden joyous 'turn'" known as the *eucatastrophe.* Tolkien coins the term by attaching the Greek prefix for "good" to the Greek word for the "down turn" of the plot. In building this paradox, he adheres to Aristotle both in his terminology and in his belief that different genres have their respective potentials. Tragedy can effect a catharsis in the spectator; the eucatastrophic fairy tale "can give to child or man that hears it, when the 'turn' comes, a catch of breath, a beat and lifting of the heart, near to (or indeed accompanied by) tears, as keen as that given by any form of literary art, and having a peculiar quality." In both cases, the effect "depends on the whole story which is the setting of the turn."[8] I emphasize the sheer physicality of the response that Tolkien has in mind to make the point that he, like Aristotle, wants to engage the human body. Tolkien is mimetic, full-bodied, robust. The modernist is not. Modernism only rarely excites emotion in the body; typically, the modernist tends toward disembodied experience—Eliot's "patient etherised upon a table"—streams of consciousness and ironic apperception. Because they are not plot-centered, novelists like Joyce and Woolf seldom move the body to strong emotion, though they are intensely rewarding in their way.

In making his case for fantasy, Tolkien bumps into Coleridge's theory of imagination. Like Eliot (whose comments on the subject precede Tolkien's by only a few years), Tolkien will not allow Coleridge's absolute distinction, in terms of faculties of mind, between a lower fancy and a higher imagination. It will be helpful to have at hand the critical passage from Coleridge, from chapter 13 of the *Biographia Literaria:*

> The Imagination then I consider either as primary, or secondary. The primary imagination I hold to be the living power and prime agent of all human perception, and as a repetition in the finite mind of the eternal act of creation in the infinite I AM. The secondary I consider as an echo of the former, coexisting with the conscious will,

8. Aristotle, *The Basic Works of Aristotle,* 1461 (*Poetics* 1450a); J. R. R. Tolkien, *Poems and Stories,* 175, 176.

yet still as identical with the primary in the kind of its agency, and differing only in degree, and in the mode of its operation. It dissolves, diffuses, dissipates, in order to re-create; or where this process is rendered impossible, yet still at all events it struggles to idealize and to unify. It is essentially vital, even as all objects (*as* objects) are essentially fixed and dead.

Fancy, on the other hand, has no other counters to play with, but fixities and definites. The fancy is indeed no other than a mode of memory emancipated from the order of time and space; and blended with, and modified by that empirical phenomenon of the will, which we express by the word choice. But equally with the ordinary memory it must receive all its materials ready made from the law of association.[9]

Eliot responds by confessing his ignorance of Coleridge's sources in Hegel, Fichte, and Schelling. He then comments, "Hence it may be that I wholly fail to appreciate this passage." But poets have more crotchets than a dowager's kitty-cat. The philosophy is a red herring (that should get rid of the kitty); the real issue is Coleridge's Prometheanism, to which Eliot is actually less receptive than Tolkien is. Eliot and Tolkien agree that Coleridge's Imagination-Fancy distinction is arbitrary. Eliot chooses to underscore the importance of memory in imagination, and therefore "the importance of instinctive and unconscious, as well as deliberate selection."[10] Tolkien chooses to delimit imagination to the power of image-making, and to use *fantasy* (which is a forebear of the younger word *fancy*) to describe the art linking imagination to "Sub-creation."

Beyond nomenclature, what are the real differences between Tolkien and Coleridge? Coleridge in his theorizing about literature is more psychological and introspective. To those who sit at the feet of STC, "the art of fantasy" is not pleonastic; "the art of imagination" is, and therefore it sounds like an advertising slogan. Tolkien, like the mole in the romantic garden, is contesting romantic sensibilities at the etymological level. And yet the assumption of creative powers is much the same in either case, be it fantasy or imagination. "For my present purpose," writes Tolkien, "I require a word which shall embrace both

9. Coleridge, *Oxford Authors*, 313.
10. Eliot, *Use of Poetry*, 68, 69.

the Sub-creative Art in itself and a quality of strangeness and wonder in the Expression, derived from the Image." Strangeness, wonder, and image are no strangers to Coleridge's tree, and it would be tempting to dismiss Tolkien as cranky and unoriginal. He wants to avoid "technical not normal language"—a knock, I think, at Coleridge and his critical heirs, like Cambridge professor I. A. Richards. More important, he objects to Coleridge's argument that supernatural stories elicit a "willing suspension of disbelief." "What really happens," writes Tolkien, "is that the story-maker proves a successful 'sub-creator.' He makes a Secondary World which your mind can enter. Inside it, what he relates is 'true': it accords with the laws of that world."[11] One gains an insight into Tolkien's stubborn character and outlook from the fact that the author of "On Fairy-Stories" never once mentions Coleridge by name.

A romantic Catholic, Tolkien and his cause were defeated at the Battle of Culloden, and Coleridge proceeded to set the "technical" terms of culture. And so we trace an encounter that resembles an ancient wound. Tolkien adopts from Coleridge the terms *primary* and *secondary* to describe the real world and the created world of the literary artist: he uses these terms with respect to the Primary World of God and the Secondary World of the writer, whereas Coleridge speaks of the Primary Imagination of man and the Secondary Imagination of the poet. But even if we sense the burden of Tolkien's historical self-consciousness, including his relation to Coleridge, yet Tolkien does not deconstruct himself or wallow in his status as victim. He commits himself to a bold theological proposition that inspired Coleridge's best poetry and worst nightmares. Coleridge was highly sensitive to heresy. We have encountered his thinking on humanism, and ironic it would be if Coleridge proved to be the vessel of what he abhors. At issue is the romantic poet's divine aspiration. To anybody approaching Tolkien with a knowledge of English romanticism, it is plain to see that Middle-earth shares a border with Coleridge's Xanadu. To revisit the prefatory note to "Kubla Khan" is to mark just the correspondence between images and things that underlies Tolkien's fantasy.[12]

11. Tolkien, *Poems and Stories,* 155, 146.
12. "In the summer of the year 1797, the Author, then in ill health, had retired to a lonely farm house between Porlock and Linton, on the Exmoor confines of

Coleridge needed the pretext of an opium-inspired dream for his Prometheanism, that is, for arrogating to himself the power of creation and rewriting Genesis. Tolkien likewise makes a world and rewrites Genesis. Then, bold creature, he goes a step farther and subcreates salvation:

> in the "eucatastrophe" we see in a brief vision . . . a far-off gleam or echo of *evangelium* in the real world. The use of this word . . . is a serious and dangerous matter. It is presumptuous of me to touch on such a theme; but if by grace what I say has in any respect any validity, it is, of course, only one facet of a truth incalculably rich: finite only because the capacity of Man for whom this was done is finite.[13]

This humble boldness would have shocked Coleridge. If, as Chesterton suggested, English Romanticism was the French Revolution translated in greater glory to the field of imagination, Tolkien stages a Catholic Uprising translated in greater glory to the Field of Cormallen.

At root, the metaphysical assumptions of Catholicism differ from those of English Protestantism. Coleridge and the romantic movement are, in consequence, forced to steal the power of heaven, while Catholics are at home in a world of sacramental miracles. The romantic imagination is militant; the Catholic imagination is daring. These differences account for Tolkien's ending his lecture with a metaphysical optimism unknown to modern literature since Shakespeare's romances:

Somerset and Devonshire. In consequence of a slight disposition, an anodyne had been prescribed, from the effects of which he fell asleep in his chair at the moment that he was reading the following sentence, or words of the same substance, in 'Purchas's Pilgrimage': 'Here the Khan Kubla commanded a palace to be built, and a stately garden thereunto. And thus ten miles of fertile ground were enclosed within a wall.' The author continued for about three hours in a profound sleep, at least of the external senses, during which time he has the most vivid confidence, that he could not have composed less than from two hundred to three hundred lines; if that indeed can be called composition in which *all the images rose up before him as things,* with a parallel production of the correspondent expressions, without any sensation or consciousness of effort" (Coleridge, *Oxford Authors,* 102 [italics mine]).

13. Tolkien, *Poems and Stories,* 178.

The Christian has still to work, with mind as well as body, to suffer, hope, and die; but he may now perceive that all his bents and faculties have a purpose, which can be redeemed. So great is the bounty with which he has been treated that he may now, perhaps, fairly dare to guess that in Fantasy he may actually assist in the effoliation and multiple enrichment of creation. All tales may come true; and yet, at the last, redeemed, they may be as like and as unlike the forms we give them as Man, finally redeemed, will be like the fallen that we know.[14]

The passage is emblematic of Tolkien's work, which expresses a fine theological rapprochement between his Augustinian sense of our fallenness and his Thomistic confidence in our "bents and faculties." Tolkien is acutely aware of the fall of man, but his humanism goes deeper than Coleridge's Prometheanism or than Eliot's tolerant spirit and civilized tone. He is more optimistic regarding human potential, and more emotional about human tragedy. He is much closer to Chesterton, citing "Chestertonian Fantasy" with approval, though remarking, "it has, I think, only a limited power; for the reason that recovery of freshness of vision is its only virtue." I am not sure that this "only" is fair to the author of *The Man Who Was Thursday,* an almost Kafka-esque nightmare that dovetails into a waking dream of pure joy.[15] And there is no real justification for making *fantasy* a permanent alternative to *imagination.* Chesterton's novels are highly imaginative romances set in the real world. They procure a "willing suspension of disbelief." But Tolkien is surely right to connect Chesterton to Dickens. They recover the fantastic element in modern life, while Tolkien is more respectful of reality than the term *fantasy* would usually suggest.[16]

In his secondary world, Tolkien conserves reason and nature from their abuse by a despotic modernity. He describes fantasy as "a rational not an irrational activity."[17] Its "natural" wholesomeness is inseparable from reason:

14. Ibid., 180.

15. Ibid., 166. For Chesterton and Kafka, see C. S. Lewis, "Notes on the Way"; and Garry Wills, *Chesterton: Man and Mask,* 49–50.

16. For a learned discussion of the fate of fantasy as a genre, see Verlyn Flieger, "What Good Is Fantasy?"

17. Tolkien, *Poems and Stories,* 156n1.

Fantasy is a natural human activity. It certainly does not destroy or even insult Reason; and it does not either blunt the appetite for, nor obscure the perception of, scientific verity. On the contrary. The keener and clearer is the reason, the better fantasy will it make. If men were ever in a state in which they did not want to know or could not perceive truth (facts or evidence), then Fantasy would languish until they were cured. If they ever get into that state (it would not seem at all impossible), Fantasy will perish, and become Morbid Delusion.[18]

Because the findings of empirical science satisfy our inborn hunger for truth, fantasy must respect those findings, for if it betrays human nature it will "languish" and "perish." But let us reverse the proposition: what does fantasy have to say when men betray human nature? Tolkien in his lecture makes grim reference to the misery imposed by "the Führer's or any other Reich."[19] The tyrant seizes control of reason and nature; he injures or destroys them. For the writer of fantasy in a tyrannical regime, two possibilities follow. Somewhat like our contemporary purveyors of "dark fantasy," he will succumb to "Morbid Delusion." Or he will protect reason and nature, seeing them as necessary guides to the good life. When they are suppressed by tyranny, he conserves the experience of what happiness looks and feels like.

It is a salient fact of modern life that myth and science have parted company. The seventeenth century was the last time when first-rate intellects could imagine a synthesis of all knowledge, with Christianity at its center. Western man has been a Cartesian being ever since. Religion, we say, speaks to his heart and science speaks to his mind. Or else it might be the other way around: religion saves his mind and science saves his body. In either case he remains split—a condition that may prove fatal.

If we are sensitive to this dilemma, we are likely to feel that modernity neglects the deepest truths because the idol of science demands it. Tolkien, who never denigrates the good of science, is an empiricist aware that empiricism has its limits. What he objects to is believing that the transient products of the assembly line "are more 'real' than, say, horses." The instant world of technology cannot relate truth to

18. Ibid., 162.
19. Ibid., 168.

goodness and beauty; it is all too likely to generate "unreason" and to impoverish history. Science becomes irrational when it seizes authority over history and culture: "For it is after all possible for a rational man . . . to arrive at the condemnation implicit at least in the mere silence of 'escapist' literature, of progressive things like factories, or the machine-guns and bombs that appear to be their most natural and inevitable, dare we say 'inexorable,' products." Real progress is not "the march of science," and we mimic the fatal logic of "mass-production robot factories" if we think it is. Man is degraded by scientism: "by the hypotheses (or dogmatic guesses) of scientific writers who classed Man not only as 'an animal'—that correct classification is ancient—but as 'only an animal.'"[20]

It is helpful to recall on just what grounds Chesterton accepted evolution. He agreed that evolution could have produced man and ape: "But if it means anything more, it means that there is no such thing as an ape to change, and no such thing as a man for him to change into. It means that there is no such thing as a thing." That answer will, I think, prove more satisfying to the Platonist than to the pragmatist. But there is more. In *The Everlasting Man,* Chesterton reflected on the distinct strangeness of the human mind: "It was not and it was; we know not in what instant or in what infinity of years. Something happened; and it has all the appearance of a transaction outside of time."[21] Chesterton's position is a study in reasonableness. To ignore the deep questions about the mysterious nature of the mind is to indulge in a luxury that civilization cannot afford. The necessary virtues cannot survive the erosion of free will.

Nor can the arts. Tolkien alludes to Darwin in a sympathetic quotation of Christopher Dawson: "'The rawness and ugliness of modern European life'—that real life whose contact we should welcome—'is the sign of a biological inferiority, of an insufficient or false reaction to environment.'" The ugliness around us, from LA to London, indicates social failure and ignorance of reality. As Dawson remarks, a civilization "out of touch with the life of nature and of human nature as well" may produce "a kind of grim Assyrian beauty."[22] The Assyrians lived under the desert sun of despotism. Their art was typically "direct,

20. Ibid., 170, 187.
21. Chesterton, *Collected Works,* 1:238, 2:170.
22. Dawson, quoted in Tolkien, *Poems and Stories,* 171, 171n1.

aggressive, masculine, unsubtle, power-obsessed, like their kings."[23] By contrast, Tolkien's comments on architecture recall Pugin, Ruskin, Chesterton, and the Gothic revival: "In Faërie one can indeed conceive of an ogre who possesses a castle hideous as a nightmare. . . , but one cannot conceive of a house built with a good purpose—an inn, a hostel for travelers, the hall of a virtuous and noble king—that is yet sickeningly ugly. At the present day it would be rash to hope to see one that was not—unless it was built before our time." The ogre is a despot, and his castle reflects his ignoble rule. So it is not just that the best fairy-stories have an "inherent morality."[24] It is that the "inner consistency" of these tales is a sign of health, so that goodness and beauty and truth can go hand in hand, like the graces dancing.

Tolkien is not a primitivist, he is a revolutionary. He calls our period "the Robot Age" insofar as science has been co-opted by the will to power, alienating man from reason and nature. He expressly connects his authorship of fantasy to the possibility of insurrection. Fantasy is therefore related to radical Christian politics. Like Chesterton, who expressed a nuanced, Christian sympathy for the French Revolution, Tolkien maintains his right to rise up against tyranny and to rescue modern man from the threat of brainwashed degradation. The very idea of technological power as personal empowerment is an aspect of that brainwashing with which Tolkien takes issue. The Hobbits experience a moral education with respect to power and its uses. Bilbo does not seize a magical object and use it to rise in status. Heeding Gandalf's counsel, Frodo leaves the Ring alone for a long time. Sam has the moral strength to return the Ring to Frodo. In sum, Middle-earth is not a video game, a technological playground for the savage ego to smash things. It is a place where wisdom, tradition, and rightly ordered hierarchies nourish different cultures.

It is no accident that the question of power, its origins and uses, is central to modernity as well as to Tolkien. We can assume power with a good or a bad conscience, as Prometheans or Christians or nihilists. The nihilist is usually tortured by his conscience; otherwise he would not be anything so pretentious as a nihilist. We can be wise stewards of creation, or we can be tyrants over nature, and thrive or suffer accord-

---

23. Paul Johnson, *Art: A New History,* 37.
24. Tolkien, *Poems and Stories,* 172, 127.

ingly. These choices are at the heart of the poem that Tolkien referred to as "the leit-motif of *The Lord of the Rings*":[25]

> Three Rings for the Elven-kings under the sky,
>> Seven for the Dwarf-lords in their halls of stone,
> Nine for Mortal Men doomed to die,
>> One for the Dark Lord on his dark throne
> In the Land of Mordor where the Shadows lie.
>> One Ring to rule them all, One Ring to find them,
>> One Ring to bring them all and in the darkness bind them
> In the land of Mordor where the Shadows lie.[26]

The tone has much in common with Poe, Dowson, and Eliot, poets whose use of haunting incantation builds up a dreamlike ambience of shadow and loss. It is not so far from "The Hollow Men." The key effects are internal rhyme, end rhyme, assonance, and alliteration. Tolkien maximizes the force of the vowels, which is especially intense in the long *o*'s and the long *i*'s. The verse is all along expressing its own spellbinding power of sound, with rhymes that "find" and "bind," when the menacing repetition of "One Ring" brings the union of form and content to its onomatopoeic perfection. This is impersonal art with a vengeance, appropriate for a dark aesthetic and the technology of Sauron. The tripling of "One" in lines six and seven suggests an anti-Trinitarianism, a reaction against the Trinitarian idea, which Chesterton called "the image of a council at which mercy pleads as well as justice, the conception of a sort of liberty and variety existing even in the inmost chamber of the world."[27] This liberty and variety are just what Sauron negates. As evil personified, Sauron takes shape in answer to our *mortal* fears, which are alluded to by "Mortal Men" and in the character of Mordor, whose name evokes murder and mortality in many languages, as the *OED* attests. Sauron's spell achieves what appears to be death's absolute binding power, which is overcome only through the Passion and the Resurrection. It is nearly overcome by Frodo, who begins to realize what Saint Paul in his Letter to the Ephesians calls "the measure of the full

25. J. R. R. Tolkien, *The Letters of J. R. R. Tolkien,* 153.

26. Tolkien, *Fellowship of the Ring,* 3.

27. Chesterton, *Collected Works,* 1:340.

stature of Christ" (4:13 *NRSV*). To choose the dark power is to surrender to our fear and to relinquish our best potential. It is to merge our will with the Ring's instrumental power, and so to deny freedom and natural law. It is to despair at the most merciless of fates, in that Sauron represents a form of theological despotism, in which the appearances of the common sunlit world give way to shadows, and there is no escape from the nightmare.

Tolkien's genius in symbolizing fate is, in our time, how the *Beowulf* poet "asserts his immortality";[28] it has been lost on critics who cannot imagine a living myth. All myth gives a form to fate, making it less terrifying. From the day that Bilbo finds the Ring, it compels the characters to deal with it, and to do so in general darkness. The riddle game ("Riddles in the Dark") between Bilbo and Gollum, where Bilbo slightly cheats, or bends the rules to win and survive, is an epitome of the Ring's taking hold. It is a revelation of fate or doom, limiting the field of freedom to almost nothing. Aristotle says the essence of a riddle is "to describe a fact in an almost impossible combination of words."[29] Fate itself is the eternal riddle, which time illuminates. Time is of course what Gollum runs out of. And time, very much time, gives an answer to Bilbo's final riddle that we could not possibly have guessed. In their epic scale, the works of Middle-earth give us time's answers in the mythological form of subcreation.

We can, I think, begin to appreciate Tolkien's "fairy-story" as an act of "[r]ecovery (which includes return and renewal of health)." It is like a wave restoring the whale to her natural element. It permits human nature, in Chesterton's phrase, "really to reveal itself as human." This bountiful satisfaction is something modernist literature cannot provide. In truth, this bountiful satisfaction is something that the aesthete cannot even comprehend. His eyes simply glaze over at Denethor's explanation to Pippin, about the descent of Boromir's horn: "And in my turn I bore it, and so did each eldest son of our house, far back into the vanished years before the failings of the kings, since Vorondil father of Mardil hunted the wild kine of Araw in the far fields of Rhûn."[30] What we see here is the past becoming present, a form of mythic history that

28. Eliot, *Sacred Wood,* 48.
29. Aristotle, *Basic Works,* 1478 (*Poetics* 1458a28).
30. Tolkien, *Poems and Stories,* 165; Chesterton, *Victorian Age,* 107; J. R. R. Tolkien, *The Return of the King,* 27.

dispossesses the self of its selfishness and makes possible both tragedy and eucatastrophe. Unbeknownst to Denethor, the breaking of the steward's horn heralds the return of the king. True, Eliot had introduced the "mythical method" as a way of organizing history, but that highly cerebral method did not do justice to human nature. Inspired by *Ulysses,* it was expressly directed against narrative. Tolkien refuses Eliot and the modernist movement through his anthropocentric intensity, his Christian devotion to the earthly creature whose story takes place under the eucatastrophic stars of creation.

Chesterton described the history of pagan mythology as an imaginative seeking after truth. It was a kind of faith seeking understanding, and its culmination was the literal birth of Jesus, in whom faith finds understanding. Christianity, Chesterton writes in *The Everlasting Man,* is "the realisation both of mythology and philosophy." The soul of Christendom is "common sense." *The Everlasting Man* informs Tolkien's remark, "Something really 'higher' is occasionally glimpsed in mythology: Divinity, the right to power (as distinct from its possession), the due of worship; in fact 'religion.'" Like Chesterton, Tolkien aims to unite myth to reason and nature. *The Silmarillion* and *The Lord of the Rings* are therefore, in this significant respect, less primitivist than *Der Ring des Nibelungen* or *The Waste Land.* Tolkien writes myth as an analogue of Christianity. Likewise, Christianity suffuses Tolkien's real-life sense of history, which "often resembles 'Myth,' because they are both ultimately of the same stuff." This conclusion looks to be of a piece with more recent theories of narrative history.[31] The difference is that Tolkien makes us aware of the structure of history, without effectively reducing that structure to what we can say about it. For Tolkien, the mysterious (ultimately Christian) teleology of human nature and its corollary, mimetic art, supply a common ground for history in any age.

The Lord of the Rings is an apology for Christian humanism in the historically emerging sense that is the central concern of this book.[32] Tolkien's fantasy is not so much an escape from modernity as a rejection of modern dehumanization. As such, it relates truth to goodness

---

31. Chesterton, *Everlasting Man,* 251, 276; Tolkien, *Poems and Stories,* 136, 140. For a rival view of the relation of myth to history, see Hayden White, *The Content of the Form: Narrative Discourse and Historical Representation.*

32. I am preceded in my placement of Tolkien as a Christian humanist by the helpful discussion in Birzer, *J. R. R. Tolkien's Sanctifying Myth,* 133–36.

to beauty, in an analogue of Christian myth that tells the story of man in the created order.

The trilogy is also an example of the humanist's traditional devotion to authors and their books. In this respect Tolkien's framework— the prologue and the appendices—rewards close attention. The appendices are the work of an accomplished humanist. Dead languages are lovingly revived, with analyses of pronunciation and a discourse on translation. There is an explicit analogy between "the fair elven-tongue" and Latin: "The High-elven Quenya has been spelt as much like Latin as its sounds allowed."[33] Ancient histories are recorded, annals of kings and rulers, with genealogies and calendars.

Tolkien's device for gathering this abundant wealth of lore and learning, as well as *The Hobbit* and *The Lord of the Rings,* is the fabled Red Book of Westmarch, which includes a trove of poems and songs and maps.[34] The Red Book is, in effect, a tribute to the selfless labor of scribes. Its fortuitous existence recalls, for example, how the *scriptorium* of Saint Martin of Tours saved Livy in the eighth century. A single essential copy of a fifth-century text is all that survived:

> The original Red Book has not been preserved, but many copies were made, especially of the first volume, for the use of the descendants of the children of Master Samwise. The most important copy, however, has a different history. It was kept at Great Smials, but it was written in Gondor, probably at the request of the great-grandson of Peregrin, and completed in S.R. 1592 (F.A. 172). Its scribe appended this note: Findegil, King's Writer, finished this work in IV 172. It is an exact copy in all details of the Thain's book in Minas Tirith. That book was a copy, made at the request of King Elessar, of the Red Book of the Periannath, and brought to him by the Thain Peregrin when he retired to Gondor in IV 64.
>
> The Thain's book was thus the first copy made of the Red Book and contained much that was later omitted or lost. In Minas Tirith it received much annotation, and many corrections, especially of names, words, and quotations in the Elvish languages; and there was added to it an abbreviated version of those parts of *The Tale of*

---

33. Tolkien, *Return of the King,* 391.
34. This was a favorite device of Tolkien's. Compare the Book of Mazarbul.

Aragorn and Arwen which lie outside the account of the War. The full tale is stated to have been written by Barahir, grandson of the Steward Faramir, some time after the passing of the King. But the chief importance of Findegil's copy is that it alone contains the whole of Bilbo's "Translations from the Elvish." These three volumes were found to be a work of great skill and learning in which, between 1403 and 1418, he had used all the sources available to him in Rivendell, both living and written.[35]

Substitute "Elven" for "Latin," and the type of work described by Tolkien in his prologue and appendices might be summarized by Kristeller:

> Along with the copying and editing of Latin authors, the humanists developed the techniques of textual and historical criticism, studied Latin orthography, grammar, and rhetoric, ancient history and mythology, as well as archaeology, epigraphy, and antiquarian subjects. Finally, the humanists produced a vast body of commentaries on the various Latin authors, . . . in which they incorporated their philological and historical knowledge as well as their critical judgment.[36]

In Tolkien's hands, the work of philology broadens and deepens in scope, as if a renaissance was in the making.[37] This side of Tolkien's work can be slightly tongue-in-cheek, but the humor is wholesome. If the great myth is a work of subcreation, a fantasy whose connection to reality is indirect, Tolkien asserts his scholarly craft in the framework supporting his myth. This framework is, in effect, a humanistic meditation on the nature of scholarship, and on the uncanny grounds of its health and continuity. It is a further effort by the author—one more act of mediation and accommodation—to relate his myth to truth.

35. Tolkien, prologue to *Fellowship of the Ring,* 23–24.
36. Kristeller, *Renaissance Thought,* 15.
37. For Tolkien and philology, see T. A. Shippey, *The Road to Middle-earth,* 4–10.

Part III

GNOSTIC AESTHETICISM

5

ANTIHUMANISM IN BECKETT AND OTHERS

In *What's Wrong with the World,* Chesterton hits on a psychological truth about modernity:

> The brain breaks down under the unbearable virtue of mankind. There have been so many flaming faiths that we cannot hold; so many harsh heroisms that we cannot imitate; so many great efforts of monumental building or of military glory which seem to us at once sublime and pathetic. The future is a refuge from the fierce competition of our forefathers. The older generation, not the younger, is knocking at our door.[1]

Chesterton's suggestion would be taken up by critical eminences of a later time. Walter Jackson Bate appeared to be breaking new ground when he wrote: "We would . . . argue that the remorseless deepening of self-consciousness, before the rich and intimidating legacy of the past, has become the greatest single problem that modern art . . . has had to face, and that it will become increasingly so in the future."[2] Harold Bloom, whom I reserve for the next chapter, appeared to be stealing his *Anxiety of Influence* from Bate. Why the gap of sixty-odd years between Chesterton's insight and Bloom's juggernaut? Because the high modernists arrived—unforeseen by Chesterton. Tolkien excepted, they were the last of the monumental builders, the last to seize the heights of western culture. Their effort was apocalyptic, a radical individualizing of religion, a discarding of the older social ideals that Chesterton called "the unfinished temple." Their works are a prelude to postmodernism's

1. G. K. Chesterton, *What's Wrong with the World,* 29–30.
2. W. Jackson Bate, *The Burden of the Past and the English Poet,* 4.

desire to bury the past, but their artistic discipline, psychological depth, and mastery of the tradition give weight to their bid for canonical status.

The last of his kind, Samuel Beckett concluded modernism by waging total war on western culture. His answer to the spiritual breakdown and apocalyptic violence of the West is therefore opposite that of Chesterton, Eliot, and Tolkien, who try to rally constructive forces. I must plead guilty to having considerable respect for this grim son of well-to-do Irish Protestants. I will resist declaring my love for him, for that would be to acquiesce to Beckett's sentimentality: of all the geniuses lying under earth, it is Beckett who calls out most strangely to be loved. An extremely formidable and witty writer, he never shunned the western canon out of laziness or exhaustion. He knew Dante the way Keats knew Spenser. Steeped in European language, painting, and music, he possessed an imposing logical intellect, which he deployed to powerful effect in his art. He is an iconoclastic mystic, whose main use of reason is to smash it. Throughout a courageous life, he contemplated the soul. Though he is the mortal foe of the Aristotelian and the Thomist, he is a writer of conscience, whose Augustinian rigor will touch the heart (and the funny bone) of many a melancholy churchman. His work is a monumental epitaph for the *author,* in the medieval sense of *auctores,* standard authors through whom the early humanists linked pagan classics to Christian classics, and the little works of man to the great works of God.

Beckett the artist is the ultimate aesthete, regarding style itself as outmoded. He overthrows the stylistic revolution of Joyce, for example, in a counterrevolution that accelerates the destructive logic of the aesthetic movement, which is armed against nostalgia. Consider the thoughts of F. X. Camier, a "private investigator": "They were perhaps not so much reflections as a dark torrent of brooding where past and future merged in a single flood and closed, over a present for ever absent. Ah well." This comical allusion to Joyce's stream-of-consciousness technique has Camier's past and future being absorbed into oblivion. Beckett draws on Book XI of *The Confessions* (when time "is present it has no duration") to suggest that Joyce's manner has become a cliché, a habit, a dead metaphor obscuring the Void while prolonging the illusions of identity.[3] Abandoning Joycean abundance

3. Samuel Beckett, *Mercier and Camier,* 32; Augustine, *Confessions,* 266.

in favor of stark introspective rigor, Beckett makes use of absurd systematic repetition in order to somehow "go on." These repetitions, which comment on our psychological mechanisms and drives, convey a vision of life and art as cruelly absurd if bleakly humorous. For Beckett, life and art are unrelated except through the dark illuminations of failure. Debunking the humanistic aspirations of culture, he is the prophet and martyr of "anti-art." In his leap of faith to the unknown, he desecrates the monuments of tradition and solves Chesterton's dilemma by mocking it.

Certainly there are other major figures among the antihumanists, and we may pause to consider them. In his 1996 lecture "A Catholic Modernity?" philosopher Charles Taylor describes antihumanism as "the revolt from within unbelief, as it were, against the primacy of life." Taylor argues: "the most influential proponent of this kind of view is undoubtedly Nietzsche. And it is significant that the most important antihumanist thinkers of our time: for example, Foucault, Derrida, behind them, Bataille, all draw heavily on Nietzsche." This cultural movement is one in which Beckett had a hand. His friend and publisher John Calder observes of Beckett's work: "time and again he targets parents as irresponsible criminals." Adds Calder: "In private I knew Beckett to express a passive anger at those who insisted on having families, however gloomy the future outlook, but in everyday life it is not possible to be both honest and logical in front of others who don't think about such things in terms of consequences and take a conventional view of life as a 'gift.'" So I agree with Taylor that antihumanism "has been an important stream in our culture."[4] And I agree, more generally, that benevolent secular universalism lacks the conviction to inspire the good will it professes, and that this lack makes for a very sorry spectacle.

But I wonder if Taylor slightly exaggerates the influence of philosophy. The philosophical background is absolutely essential to cultural history, of course, but it usually remains a background. It is more often religion and the arts that serve as a conduit, transporting the philosopher's ideas to the busy avenues and bustling centers of culture. Taylor mentions literature with respect to only the French poets Charles Baudelaire (whose antihumanism Taylor is undecided about) and

4. Charles Taylor, *A Catholic Modernity?* 24, 25; John Calder, *The Philosophy of Samuel Beckett,* 131; Taylor, *Catholic Modernity?* 24.

Stéphane Mallarmé. The case of Baudelaire is famously ambiguous; Eliot, for instance, understood Baudelaire as classicist and Catholic. And it is doubtful that the symbolist poet Mallarmé, who described his own work as "a labyrinth illuminated by flowers,"[5] rivals the influence of Baudelaire. Certainly the origins of antihumanism precede Beckett; but as a novelist and playwright he is the one who brings antihumanism home to western consciousness. My guess is that more people have seen or read *Waiting for Godot* than have read Nietzsche.

Having plucked philosophy by the beard, I now propose to devote several pages to Beckett's philosophical background. The main influence is Schopenhauer. With the fine hypodermic of his prose, Schopenhauer injected eastern fatalism into the western bloodstream. More specifically, he combined some of the darker strains of eastern religion with Kantian epistemology. He locked the world in a prison of illusion, behind which stood not the undifferentiated reality of Brahman but an insidious metaphysical nightmare. He identified the unknowable Kantian noumenon or thing-in-itself with the Cosmic Will: the motive force of a timeless and impersonal cosmos. In the cheery view of Schopenhauer, we inhabit a world of space and time and causality that exists only in our heads. The truth is outside our forms of thought: it is the appalling Cosmic Will, which shackles us with desires and ensnares us in falsehood. Schopenhauer describes a small number of saints who break the illusions of the Will and eventually "will otherwise."[6] But in our usual state, the ego is bad, to live is to suffer, and Original Sin is just being born. Unfortunately, the best we can hope for is to escape the world and achieve personal extinction.

The overlap with gnosticism is extensive. Schopenhauer is unusual among major philosophers not only for addressing gnosticism but for liking it. The gnostics teach "pessimism and asceticism," he writes, "abstinence of every kind, but especially from all sexual satisfaction."[7] I pass over the archaeological limits of Schopenhauer's understanding. What matters is that he applauds the gnostics for their general dissent from the "optimistic history of creation" found in Genesis: "And God saw all that he had made, and behold it was very good."

---

5. Mallarmé, quoted and translated by Arthur Symons, *The Symbolist Movement in Literature,* 62.
6. Arthur Schopenhauer, *The World as Will and Representation,* 2:646.
7. Ibid., 2:620.

Schopenhauer's sense of space and time as instruments of the Cosmic Will fits perfectly with the gnostic belief that creation itself was a fall. Most important, Schopenhauer resurrects ancient heresies while he attacks the orthodox. He is anti-Christian, to be sure, but he appears to have escaped censure by being comparatively more anti-Semitic— for example, by blaming the Jews for those misplaced notes of "optimism" in the New Testament.

Schopenhauer liked good wine and a fine supper, but he did not subordinate art to nature (as he might expect his chef to do). He wanted art to lift the veil of appearances, and therefore to free the intellect for contemplation. He said it was music, of all the arts, that best answers the question, "What is life?" for music best expresses "the innermost nature of all life and existence." Most especially, music reveals the truth about "sexual love," which for Schopenhauer is the central theme of art and "the ultimate goal of almost all human effort."[8] It follows that Schopenhauer is a skeptic about romance. He thinks that the Cosmic Will lays a trap for lovers, in the form of the pathos and sublimity of love. Our romantic ideals actually serve the Cosmic Will, which lures men and women together in order to renew the species. (Q. Why would the Cosmic Will do such a thing? A. To satisfy its Baal-like craving for an ideal baby.)

Schopenhauer's influence is palpable in Wagner's *Tristan und Isolde,* one of the most important operas of the nineteenth century and much darker in tone than the tragic romance of Aragorn and Arwen. The gist of the story is this: Tristan is a knight escorting the Irish princess Isolde by ship to England, where she is to marry King Mark. Isolde formerly nursed Tristan back to health, but now she is indignant over her forced marriage to King Mark, and furious at Tristan, who has slain her intended husband in combat, and whose resulting wounds inspired the act of compassion that she now regrets. She plots to poison Tristan and herself, but her attendant substitutes a love philter for the poison. After Tristan and Isolde drink the fateful cup, hate erupts into love, free will evaporates, and tragedy engulfs the young pair. Baudelaire observed in Wagner's orchestration "an absolute, despotic taste for a dramatic ideal,"[9] an apt description of music that glorifies passionate

8. Ibid., 2:620, 533.
9. Charles Baudelaire, *The Painter of Modern Life and Other Essays,* 122.

suffering without understanding. The lovers in Wagner's opera are drowned by their emotions. Their fate is cruel. Their minds succumb to magic while the audience marvels at the sublimity of passion.

To follow Schopenhauer's corruption of the European mind is to chart the growth of modern antihumanism. Through Wagner, at least, Schopenhauer impacts Nietzsche's landmark early work *The Birth of Tragedy.* Nietzsche quotes Wagner's remark that civilization is "nullified by music just as lamplight is nullified by the light of day." Civilization, nature, and all individuals are locked in illusion, the Indic maya or magic, which Nietzsche identifies with the bright world of Apollo. By contrast, Dionysus inspires tragedy, "the shattering of the individual and his fusion with primal being."[10] Wagner, Laforgue, Hardy, Wilde, Conrad, Beckett: all owe more of their ideas to Schopenhauer than to Kant or Hegel. Combining superior taste with a subversive force of personality, Schopenhauer is the anti-Apollonian oracle of old Europe's slow suicide. His gnostic aestheticism undoes all humanistic values. He opens a path for the fatalism of the Orient to return like Dionysus, conquering the cities of Europe. He sickens western culture with a sense that reality is neither good nor real, that human nature lacks permanence and depth, that Christianity is, in Marx's poisonous phrase, the opiate of the masses. Art offers a crumb of salvation because it makes us conscious of our sexually monstrous selves. So conceived, art moves historically in an antihumanist direction, away from mimesis, away from the pure aesthetic harmonies of Kant, toward a shuddering recognition of the heart of darkness.

Chesterton wrongly believed that western civilization had outgrown Schopenhauer. Commenting on the origins of *The Man Who Was Thursday,* he looked back on fin-de-siècle aestheticism:

> The people who read Schopenhauer regarded themselves as having found out everything and found that it was nothing. Their system was a system, and therefore had a character of surrounding the mind. It therefore really resembled a nightmare, in the sense of being imprisoned or even bound hand and foot; of being none the less captive because it was rather in a lunatic asylum than a reasonable hell or place of punishment. There is a great deal in the modern world

---

10. Friedrich Nietzsche, *Basic Writings of Nietzsche,* 59, 65.

that I think evil and a great deal more that I think silly; but it does seem to me to have escaped from this mere prison of pessimism.[11]

Chesterton wrote these words in 1926, after *The Waste Land* had mesmerized the young. He appears to have underestimated Pater's impact, and he failed to notice that Schopenhauer's ideas were passing from the aesthetic movement to its modernist heirs. "The cult of suicide committed suicide sometime ago," quipped Chesterton. But the joke fell flat. In the end, Schopenhauer's influence intersected with resurgent gnostic tendencies throughout the culture, particularly in the arts and in the use of technology, to give the cult of suicide a power to rival the Church.[12]

Like Nietzsche, Eliot reflects the general influence of Schopenhauer. In *The Birth of Tragedy,* Nietzsche echoes the demigod Silenus in Sophocles's *Oedipus at Colonus:* "Oh, wretched ephemeral race, children of chance and misery, why do you compel me to tell you what it would be most expedient for you not to hear? What is best of all is utterly beyond your reach: not to be born, not to *be,* to be *nothing.* But the second best for you is—to die soon." Likewise, the deathless Sibyl of *The Waste Land:* "'What do you want?,' the boys asked. 'I want to die.'" "April is the cruellest month" because it wakes us to the painful cycle of sex and generation.[13] In his manuscripts we find that Eliot considered using Conrad ("The horror! the horror!") for the epigraph to *The Waste Land*—it would have marked another bow to Schopenhauer. The quotations from *Tristan und Isolde* in *The Waste Land* convey, by way of Wagner, Schopenhauer's sexual metaphysics. Certainly there are rival strains in *The Waste Land,* "a clatter and a chatter from within / Where fishmen lounge at noon," near "the walls / Of Magnus Martyr."[14] The

11. Chesterton, *Collected Works,* 6:470.

12. Ibid. Rémi Brague locates the gnostic premise in the modern technological task of "imposing external order upon nature." He observes: "If technology could set out to ameliorate nature, it was because nature left a lot to be desired" (Rémi Brague, *The Wisdom of the World: The Human Experience of the Universe in Western Thought,* 209). See also Voegelin, *New Science,* 107–32.

13. Nietzsche, *Basic Writings,* 42. Maybe not everyone will recognize the poem's epigraph, taken from the *Satyricon* of Petronius, and roughly translated here. I am grateful to Professor William Charron for pointing out to me the Schopenhauerian tenor of Eliot's famous line.

14. Eliot, *Collected Poems,* 63.

Wagnerian music is a comment on the sex trap that devours lilac and Lil; the apostolic fishmen intimate a Providence that is entirely in doubt. Eliot walks a fine line, for the antihumanists have always painted the Church as the enemy.

In his short story "First Love," Beckett transposes Schopenhauer's metaphysics of love from the respectable burgher to the urban vagabond. The grotesque narrator, a disheveled wandering monad, falls for the charms of a prostitute and moves into her house. He contemplates violence against the girl, but he discovers himself to be "at the mercy of an erection." The besetting irony of his condition is that he detects the sex trap but cannot resist his feverish instincts. In consequence, sex splits him in two. He is at once fornicator and voyeur. The girl's pregnancy elicits from him the bleak humor of the damned, like the addict who craves what kills him: "Look, she said, stooping over her breasts, the haloes are darkening already. I summoned up my remaining strength and said, Abort, abort, they'll blush like new." Abortion is deliverance from a life where "haloes" are demonically dark, where there are no good fathers, and where there is no reason to welcome a child. So the narrator shuns the fruits of "love." At story's end, he describes himself being tortured for his sexual acts, in constant unsuccessful flight from the baby's cries: "But as soon as I halted I heard them again, a little fainter each time, admittedly, but what does it matter, faint or loud, cry is cry, all that matters is that it should cease. For years I thought they would cease. Now I don't think so any more. I could have done with other loves perhaps. But there it is, either you love or you don't."[15] Under such brutal stars, suicide would be heroic, in the same way that abortion would be a release from suffering. Both are forms of liberation from the condition of individuality that the Cosmic Will induces, tortures, and consumes.

Beckett's most famous work, *Waiting for Godot,* is gnostic in its pseudo-Christian and anti-Christian themes. It is an expression of Christian heresy. When asked if the play was susceptible to a Christian interpretation, Beckett answered: "Yes, Christianity is a mythology with which I am perfectly familiar. So naturally I use it." In *Waiting for Godot,* he took apart the Christian cosmos piece by piece with philosophical equipment borrowed largely from Schopenhauer. There may

15. Samuel Beckett, *The Complete Short Prose, 1929–1989,* 31, 44, 45.

be other sources for the play's gnostic themes, such as Augustine's anti-Manichean writings. In any case, the gnostic machinery of *Godot* is ubiquitous. For instance, Alice Hamilton suggests that the "they" who repeatedly beat Estragon are "the Archons or Æons, set over this world by the evil Deity presiding over the material universe." She explains that Beckett "always viewed Time as a cosmic power," a reference to the punishing Æons, who "accomplish their work by way of time (æons)."[16] Likewise, she compares Pozzo to Yahweh, the creator God (and hence the "evil Deity") of our prison-world. As she suggests, the frequent gnostic themes in Beckett's other writings confirm the gist of her observations about *Godot.*

Our suffering and our love are, in Beckett's representation, analogous to the *imitatio Christi.* Estragon says of Christ: "All my life I've compared myself to him."[17] Christ in *Waiting for Godot* stands for all mankind, but not as the historical God incarnate; rather, in keeping with the gnostic Christ, our embodied selves conceal the spiritual truth. Our divinity lies elsewhere. Being stripped and dismantled, Christendom or the West appears through the barest symbols, "twilight," "a country road," and "a tree." Christianity exists in the play in order to gesture away from itself.

For Vladimir and Estragon, Chaplinesque tramps on the tragic stage, western history has ended in catastrophe: it is perpetual Good Friday and the tree is their cross. In an important book published in England in 1946, about two years before Beckett started his play, historian R. G. Collingwood argued for a "conception of history as the re-enactment of the past in the historian's mind." Collingwood thereby met the daunting challenge that modernity poses to consciousness, to study the past and sustain the burden of thought. It was a burden that inspired fear and trembling in the poet of *Gerontion,* whose tragic vision of history Beckett renders tragically absurd—doing for Eliot what Stoppard (by way of Beckett) would do for Shakespeare. The burden is just too much for Didi and Gogo, who pointedly remarks, "I'm not a historian." Like the souls in Dante's Hell, they have lost the good of the intellect. "What is terrible is to *have* thought," says Vladimir, with

16. Beckett, quoted in Calder, *Philosophy of Samuel Beckett,* 130; Alice Hamilton, "Samuel Beckett and the Gnostic Vision of the Created World," 295, 296.

17. Samuel Beckett, *Waiting for Godot: A Tragicomedy in Two Acts,* 34.

an ambiguity on *have* that enacts the pain of possessing a mind. History is grounds for despair. It is a "charnel-house." The Holocaust haunts the stage like a proprietary ghost (one of the tramps was initially given the Jewish name of Lévy). Unless Godot arrives like the Second Coming, the tramps have no way out—except possibly through the ruins of themselves. They know that their former expedients have failed them. "We should turn resolutely towards Nature," Estragon says, momentarily overlooking that the romantics, Rousseau and Wordsworth, for example, tried and failed to reach utopia through Nature. "Ah! que voulez-vous? Exactly," Vladimir replies, echoingly, to his friend's rhetorical question about desire, before lapsing into a suggestive and mysterious silence.[18]

The humanistic pursuit of truth, goodness, and beauty is interpreted by Beckett along ideological lines. In *Godot* he represents the social order with Pozzo and Lucky. Beckett conceives the pair in ways that suggest the master-slave morality envisioned by Hegel (though Beckett is no Hegelian, far from it) as a phase in the evolution of political and moral consciousness. They are symbiotic creatures who do not comprehend this central absurd fact about their existence. Believing he is made "in God's image," Pozzo never pauses to ask how it is that his "carrier" or "knook" has taught him "Beauty, grace, truth of the first water." He takes it for granted that Lucky "wants to impress me, so that I'll keep him." In other words, he does not glimpse the reality behind the social order. Not even their ruin in act 2 frees them from their prison. Pozzo's literal blindness endows his words with a prophetic insight that he characteristically fails to act upon; the resulting dramatic ironies (for example, "I woke up one fine day as blind as Fortune") intensify the mood of gnostic despair.[19]

Lucky's obscure speech, toward the end of act 1, is a fragmented revue of the wisdom of the West. After a little vaudeville shuffle, the suffering servant makes a grotesque effort at theological-philosophical-scientific synthesis. He begins with a torrent of prophetic stammer-

18. R. G. Collingwood, *The Idea of History,* 163; Beckett, *Waiting for Godot,* 42, 41, 42. The Marquis de Sade, whom Beckett certainly admired, replied to Rousseau's natural ecstasy with an ecstasy of his own. Sade's antihumanism gained much authority in the last century; maybe western civilization is declaring Sade its *genius loci.*

19. Beckett, *Waiting for Godot,* 22, 21, 55.

ing: "Given the existence as uttered forth in the public works of Puncher and Wattmann of a personal God quaquaquaqua with white beard quaquaquaqua outside time." This "personal God" lends cruel support to the punching order of Pozzo, a patriarch who resembles Yahweh, not least through his slow crucifixion of Lucky, who "carries" a type of cross. Through Lucky's routine, Beckett stages the crisis of modernity, the moment when history falls apart, that is, when man's catastrophe erupts from his own historical consciousness. Lucky sums up man ("Fartov and Belcher," "Testew and Cunard") and his metaphysics in scatological and sexual puns: "as a result of the labors left unfinished crowned by the Acacacacademy of Anthropopopometry of Essy-in-Possy of Testew and Cunard." What slips out of this paronomasia is the truth of the matter (for Beckett): the measure of man's being and potential is so much shit, balls, and cunt. This knowledge of fate is reinforced by time's punishing effects: "it is established . . . that man . . . in spite of the strides of alimentation and defecation wastes and pines . . . in spite of the strides of physical culture."[20] Without the intercession of a God who (if he exists) kills us for his sport, man is abandoned to the elements of a mortal world that recedes before his paralyzed gaze. Lucky's final word is the opposite of Christ's (according to John 19:30): "unfinished." Salvation is alien to this world. In other words, Lucky has been looking in the wrong place. His soul is lost so long as he pursues his fate as the Son of Man.

Even Beckett submits to the Roman law that culture abhors a vacuum. It is the East that has the last grim laugh. Schopenhauer found in Tibetan Buddhism a satisfying description of "the several revolutions in the destruction and regeneration of the world." The story goes that, after Brahma denied responsibility for these pointless cycles, Buddha instructed the God that "animal beings" foster "all changes in the world" through their "moral works," and that "there is no reality in the things; all is empty."[21] Drawing on Buddhism and Schopenhauer, Eliot introduced the modernist theme of egos and

20. Ibid., 28, 29.
21. Schopenhauer, *World as Will and Representation,* 2:169–70. Likewise, the ultimate "nothing," according to Schopenhauer, is "the Prajna-Paramita of the Buddhists, the 'beyond all knowledge,' in other words, the point where subject and object no longer exist" (ibid., 1:411–12).

desires locked in meaningless repetition. Playing the same changes on nothingness, repetition, and the illusions of the ego, Beckett heralds the East. Unlike Eliot, however, he is not a good European. It is true that Nietzsche contrived to make a good European of Schopenhauer;[22] but Beckett breaks the mold. *Thus Spoke Zarathustra* and *The Waste Land* are calls for cultural regeneration. *Waiting for Godot* is not. Its author is past hoping for renaissances. The choric opening line, spoken by Vladimir, negates the future: "Nothing to be done." Beckett sums up man's condition in a circular poem at the beginning of act 2 ("A dog came in the kitchen . . .") that symbolizes the dilemma of "animal beings," the revolutions of time, and the mechanism of the plot, which is meaningless.[23]

What is Beckett's point? Beckett denies the metaphysics of man, the dignity of man, and all projects that give man importance. Human nature and humanism in his work are not only unreal, they are a trap. And yet Beckett is consumed by spirit. He is a mystical ascetic who writes in the hope of gnostic grace. He is not primarily an ideologue, though ideology enters into his work. What is very refreshing about Beckett indeed is that the default position of his cosmos is mystical. The secularists do not "get" him. But his pessimism is overwhelming. His mystical quest is the opposite of Tolkien's in "Leaf by Niggle": not a joyous fulfillment of the real, but a passionless escape from the unreal. The end of this escape is not entirely clear. It is not spiritual enlightenment or nirvana; it is, I think, a compassionate, otherworldly, and mute understanding of each other's plight.

Their metaphysical yokings of East and West connect Beckett to Schopenhauer and involve them both in profound moral contradictions. Schopenhauer, the Apostle of Despair, cannot answer why he wrote four editions of his masterpiece instead of drinking hemlock. Beckett cannot answer why he became a Nobel laureate instead of an

---

22. Schopenhauer "teaches us," Nietzsche writes, "how neither riches nor honours nor erudition can lift the individual out of the profound depression he feels at the valuelessness of his existence, and how the striving after these valued things acquires meaning only through an exalted and transfiguring goal: to acquire power so as to aid the evolution of *physis* and to be for a while the corrector of its follies and ineptitudes. At first only for yourself; but through yourself in the end for everyone" (Friedrich Nietzsche, *Untimely Meditations,* 142).

23. Beckett, *Waiting for Godot,* 7, 37.

Irish nurse. For Schopenhauer and Beckett, true faith is singular and inexpressible. Yet both choose to write about it. For Schopenhauer and for Beckett, the rule of reason is oppressive. Yet both use the metaphysics of reason as a tool and a weapon.

Of course faith and reason have no easy marriage in the Christian tradition. Eliot was a Christian skeptic; granting only the basic Thomistic principle that good reasoning is not contrary to faith. The fact that Chesterton energetically defends reason, common sense, and the historical record explains why he treated "of the *praembula fidei,* those various considerations and arguments which should lead a reasonable man to the conclusion that Christianity is true."[24] Christianity can accommodate Chesterton and Eliot, different though they be.

It is reasonable to scrutinize miracles. It is reasonable to say that miracles do not happen (Arnold). It is reasonable to say that free will is a miracle (Chesterton). But the skeptic cannot assent to standards of facts and evidence, only to reject the same standards when it suits him to be more skeptical. This tactic negates dialogue. It is to resort to intellectual incoherence, changing the terms of discussion on a whim.

But pure irrationality has a power that Beckett was well aware of. Here I refer to Beckett at his most insidious, for there are moments in *Godot* when he wraps a malicious egotism in a cloak of otherworldliness. He uses the murkiness of memory to suggest that reality itself is in total crisis. This is fine. But at the same time he wants to wrangle, to take issue with historical Christianity, to mount a rationalistic challenge to the New Testament. With something like sly determination, he points out inconsistencies in the Gospels, as Vladimir begins, "Ah yes, the two thieves. Do you remember the story?" But having trained his sights on the historical Jesus, Beckett overlooks the type of reasonable conclusion from the evidence that Chesterton's Father Brown could easily have drawn. Luke is the Evangelist who (according to Vladimir) "speaks of a thief being saved." The picture that Luke suggests is that one of the thieves relented in his abuse, while the other hardened his heart. Vladimir is technically correct that "two don't

---

24. Joseph Keating, S.J., quoted by David Dooley, foreword to Chesterton, *Collected Works,* 1:33. See also my forthcoming essay, "Coming to Terms with *Four Quartets.*"

mention any thieves at all." Luke actually refers to criminals (not thieves); Matthew (27:44) and Mark (15:27) both have two thieves; John simply says "two others" (19:18), but we can hardly doubt that they were criminals in the eyes of the law. The likelihood, then, is that Luke or his source saw something the other evangelists did not see. The contradictions are apparent and not irreconcilable. It hardly takes pious juggling to suggest that Matthew, Mark, and John (or their sources), amid the crowds of Golgotha, might have been praying together or apart, or speaking to a soldier or an official, or comforting someone who was overcome with grief, when Luke heard the exchange. We can see this possibility, for instance, in Tintoretto's *Crucifixion.* Beckett was evidently loath to imagine the scene. Chasing a will-o'-wisp of logic in a fog of unbelief, he discounted the story's popular appeal. Since no one but "bloody ignorant apes" believes such nonsense, we are prodded to conspire in laughter and confirm our Pozzo-like superiority.[25]

But Pozzo's superiority is as dubious as Vladimir and Estragon's authority. We do not know what to think, and it becomes harder and harder to see the point of pointlessness. Maybe such moments are spurs to contemplation or enlightenment, if Beckett has adequately prepared us for them. Another possible lesson is that Beckett's attack on Christianity goes to the origins of the drama. The Christian myth that we see in the mystery plays, for example in the fifteenth-century York Crucifixion, has this much in common with the *Oresteia:* reason and nature and myth combine to forge a communal sense of history, with dramatic ironies breaking out like revelations in the Holy Land. The soldiers in the York Crucifixion are like Agamemnon and Clytaemnestra, oblivious to the depths at their feet. In his blindness, Pozzo likewise becomes an oracle of dramatic ironies, but his ironies deny reason and nature and history. Beckett's stammering, paralytic drama is pointedly anti-Christian. More important, it suggests the anti-Christian origins of anti-art. For it lays bare, by undoing them, the reason, nature, and history through which Christianity gives literature life.

25. Beckett, *Waiting for Godot,* 9.

6

ARTIFICIAL TASTE

Over the past decades, a dogmatically relativist type of modernism has pushed Christian humanism effectively out of the academy. At the same time, the study of literature has much declined. Neither the professors nor their students have the command of literary knowledge that flourished under the New Critics, for all their faults. Literature is of course the red meat of ideological critique, and if that was all there was to it, it might be easy for literature to survive. It could graze on the greensward before being slaughtered for the big feast during exam week. But I think there are larger and irrational forces at play, in the form of burgeoning cults. In my voyages I have seen vagina worship and the cult of feminism, the deathless cult of neo-Marxism, the dying cult of art, the death cult of antihumanism, the futuristic cult of technology, the mindless cult of wellness, the green cult of environmentalism, the media cult, and the managerial cult of multiculturalism. All hinges, in the end, on unspoken religious beliefs. And if we acknowledge these beliefs, then the thesis of this chapter will not seem incendiary or absurd: a bias against Christianity has separated literary studies from the tradition and closed off the avenues to renewal.

But the many cults of multiculturalism do not admit this thesis. Generally, their antireligious (not antispiritual!) bias forbids them to scrutinize their own religious and metaphysical premises; and each little cult has its own agenda, its own truth to inflate and extol—like a float at the Macy's Thanksgiving Day Parade. The world becomes so much simpler, in any case, when we can define traditional Christianity in terms of creationism or papal infallibility, and then placate Allah with a group hug. At best, the multiculturalists champion a "progressive" humanism that has forsaken philosophy and theology. Meanwhile, smaller movements combine to create large cultural changes. On the spiritual frontier, the vaguely Christian West is looking increasingly gnostic—the richest cults pull their floats in that direction. Technology, feminism, postmodernism, and the youth media tend to suppress the guidance of nature and reason. Literature, on the other hand, cannot wholly abandon the conditions of its birth. There is such civilized pleasure in opening a good book. It is a sensual and intellectual act that militates, like Chaucer's pilgrims themselves, against gnostic alienation. But many recent critics are gnostic in spirit; agents of the times, they have done almost everything in their unconscious and irrational power to lay the literary tradition to rest.

In retrospect, one might circle the date 1971 as a turning point. It was then that the English major entered its statistical decline: "English accounted for almost 8 percent of [undergraduate] degrees in 1971, but had sunk to 4 percent by 2002." Coincidentally, 1971 was the year when Valerie Eliot, the poet's widow, published *The Waste Land: A Facsimile and Transcript of the Original Drafts Including the Annotations of Ezra Pound.* In his brief preface, Pound remarked, "The more we know of Eliot, the better. I am thankful that the lost leaves have been unearthed."[1] Helen Hennesy Vendler began her piece in the *New York Times Book Review* (November 7, 1971) without the least trace of thankfulness. On the contrary, venom poured like honey from the hollow of her pen:

> The manuscript version of *The Waste Land,* the most famous of modern poems, is at last available. It is a version bound to raise whatever dust has settled over its celebrated lines. The poem appeared, with no notes, in October 1922, in *The Criterion;* the notorious notes, by now almost canonically part of the poem, were added to fill out the manuscript for book publication in December. By the time of his death in 1965 Eliot was, principally on account of *The Waste Land,* a culture hero, attracting thousands to his lectures. His audience were like lemmings: moving in obedience to obscure compulsions, they swarmed to hear him, filling halls to overflowing.[2]

1. Warren Goldstein, "What Would Plato Do? A (Semi-) Careerist Defense of the Liberal Arts," 38; Ezra Pound, preface to *The Waste Land: A Facsimile and Transcript of the Original Drafts,* by T. S. Eliot, vii.
2. Helen Vendler, *Part of Nature, Part of Us: Modern American Poets,* 77.

The reviewer is quick to bare her animus against the middlebrow types (students in particular) who were enthusiastic about Eliot. The crowds who came to see him were "lemmings," hero-worshipping zombies, obedient slaves of the social order. Their motives were "obscure," their independence nonexistent, their consciousness (insofar as they had any) backward and bland.

After her personal remembrance of Eliot (at seventeen—"on the floor of Harvard's unheated Memorial Hall"—she caught pneumonia), Vendler pokes away at Eliot's father, his marriage, and his mental condition. She skewers the man in order to roast the poet: "'Immature poets imitate; mature poets steal,' Eliot had written in 1920; and his thefts were on a grand scale. They formed, in fact, a principal [*sic*] of composition."[3] Vendler was pronouncing Eliot to be a massive fraud. It is worth recalling what Eliot stood for, what was at stake. Subjected to the new critical fashions were the seriousness and purpose of the liberal arts, the prestige of high culture, the reality of human greatness.

When Vendler whisks Matthew Arnold onto the stage in the role of a sexually repressed Victorian bugbear, it immediately follows that Eliot descends from Arnold: "Just as Eliot's rhythms rise from the songs in 'Empedocles on Etna,' and just as his essays find their model in Arnold's, so *The Waste Land* is the anguished poem Arnold should have written, an antiphonal duet between his aridity and his touchstones."[4] Camp or criticism, "an antiphonal duet between his aridity and his touchstones" makes a mockery of the whole comparison. The syntax has the disposable logic of a plastic world, the authority of mass production: "Just as . . . and just as . . . so. . . ." In the pages of the nation's leading newspaper, Vendler was "ranking out" two of the finest poet-critics in the language, two men who embodied the highest ideals in art.

But the critic knew her audience, who were bohemian, college-educated, and weighed down only by their disposable income. They were ironic sophisticates who could admit primitivism in the arts, but who found religion distasteful. She was confident of having the sympathy of the reader with her, to the extent that she didn't need to argue at all:

3. Ibid., 80.
4. Ibid.

The religious ending of *The Waste Land* has been so controversial for so long that it is hard to see it anew, but it certainly bears ominous overtones of what was to come in Eliot's verse, both in the preciousness of "Ash-Wednesday" ("Eliot's monument to self-pity," as Blackmur called it) and in the religiosity of *Four Quartets*. Is nervousness cured by ethics? Can "the heap of broken images" be put together again, like Humpty-Dumpty, by a heap of moral injunctions? Can Hieronymo's madness be ministered to by words from an Upanishad? To the Upanishads, in later days, Eliot added Krishna, St. John of the Cross, Blessed Julian of Norwich, and so on. And all manner of thing shall be well. But was it? Certainly not in the verse, which stretched feebler and feebler through the tracts of the *Quartets,* reposing on that unlikely poetic:

> Desiccation of the world of sense,
> Evacuation of the world of fancy,
> Inoperancy of the world of spirit.[5]

Ash-Wednesday stands as a major poem, and R. P. Blackmur's influence has shrunk to a pinprick. *Four Quartets* may be the finest long poem in English in the twentieth century. To abuse these works so recklessly ("Humpty-Dumpty"?) is to level the edifice of high culture, and to turn up one's nose at real standards. The disparaged lines reflect a theme that returns throughout Eliot's work, the *via negativa,* or dark night of the soul. It is a mystical crux that supports Eliot's theology of faith seeking understanding. The seeker must abandon what he knows; he must know failure. But Vendler is as unsympathetic as possible, a deadly vice in a critic of art. She isolates from the long poem lines that are not especially winning in themselves, but that serve the other 838 lines of the whole.

Even Shakespeare can be made to look bad, not to mention Dickens or Joyce. But modernist long poetry is a special case requiring knowledge of literary history. Eliot himself approached the problem of the modernist long poem through an analogy to music:

> Dissonance, even cacophony, has its place: just as, in a poem of any
> length, there must be transitions between passages of greater and
> less intensity, to give a rhythm of fluctuating emotion essential to

5. Ibid., 81.

the musical structure of the whole; and the passages of less intensity will be, in relation to the level on which the total poem operates, prosaic—so that, in the sense implied by that context, it may
be said that no poet can write a poem of amplitude unless he is a
master of prose.[6]

That is from Eliot's 1942 lecture "The Music of Poetry," one of his
lesser-known essays. Surely Eliot was aware of the flatness of the poetry
in question. It was a self-conscious flatness, a deliberate dull stasis,
voiding the genitive case through the failures of "of." The poetic owes
something to Pater's finest epigram: "All art constantly aspires towards
the condition of music."[7] It challenges the authority of Yeats, who
hated the prosaic qualities that Eliot brought to poetry. It is certainly
open to question. But I see Eliot's point about "fluctuating emotion,"
which is interesting in and of itself, while shedding considerable light
on *Four Quartets* and comparable works by Pound, Williams, and Jones.

The real motivation for the review, I suspect it was lost on nobody,
was to attack the standards, opinions, and careers that drew strength
and consistency from Eliot's example. It made for good theater. Vendler
was viciously haughty in delivering her *coup de grâce:* "The embarrass-
ments of the plays are beyond comment. The career tailed off more
disastrously than any other in living memory, with only sporadic lines
reminding a reader of what Eliot once had been." Philip Larkin looked
at these matters differently: "I admire *Murder in the Cathedral* as much
as anything Eliot ever wrote. I read it from time to time for pleasure,
which is the highest compliment I can pay." Geoffrey Hill admires
The Cocktail Party but condemns the last two plays.[8] Larkin and Hill
are poets, Vendler is a critic. What she lacks in talent, she makes up
for in ambitious malignity:

> The publication of these early poems, drafts, and fragments of *The
> Waste Land,* however disappointing in literary terms, can but arouse
> new commentaries which may liberate Eliot from the straitjacket

6. T. S. Eliot, *The Selected Prose of T. S. Eliot,* 112–13.

7. Pater, *Works,* 1:135.

8. Vendler, *Part of Nature,* 81–82; Philip Larkin, *Required Writing: Miscellaneous
Pieces, 1955–1982,* 66; Geoffrey Hill, "T. S. Eliot Society Memorial Lecture."

of dreary sectarian criticism: his reputation may not be enhanced in any degree, but it may take on a truer coloring. His solemn hagiographers, it is to be hoped, will be replaced by a generation of lively and unintimidated readers, quick to see his essential genius, but just as quick to see its progressive extinction.[9]

The sectarians and hagiographers, by implication unlively, intimidated, and enslaved, were to be "replaced"—like radio batteries, the Top Forty, and Western Civ. New readers of Eliot would be "quick to see his essential genius, but just as quick to see its progressive extinction." And just as quick, in their quintessential quickness, to discard the poetry altogether! After all, Eliot was a highly derivative plagiarist who somehow managed (like the fabled hundred monkeys) to write some immortal verses before turning disastrously to the theater and, worst of all, converting to Christianity.

Fast forward a quarter century. The discipline of English is incoherent. Enrollment and standards are down (way down). Wall Street is more attractive than ever to the young. And Harvard's Professor Vendler, the Dionysus of old, returns as . . . Apollo:

> The truth of the matter is that there appear, recurrently, people whose achievement in their culture is simply astonishing, each of them bringing to perfection one of humanity's talents. There is no snobbery in saying that the highest achievements in articulacy, like the highest ones in music or mathematics, are produced by very few, and those very few highly trained. . . . The real snobs are those who would, in the name of the people, deny to the people the very education the geniuses of the world—Eliot among them, as these lectures [Eliot's Clark Lectures] remind us—have to offer.[10]

Apparently, those lemmings were intelligent mammals after all. Eliot, that old stick-in-the-mud, was "one of the geniuses of the world." Abandoning her confessional style (readers of the *New York Times* swarmed to hear her), Vendler berates her professional colleagues: "care for language is in short supply among sociologically and psychologically minded critics." How true! But what were those bright young things reading in 1971?

9. Vendler, *Part of Nature,* 85.
10. Helen Vendler, review of *The Varieties of Metaphysical Poetry,* by T. S. Eliot.

Harold Bloom played opposite the diva's glass-shattering soprano in that celebrated mock-opera of the late twentieth century, "The Triumph of Decadence," where everyone is madly in love with himself. In the Sunday *New York Times* of August 21, 1977, Bloom ruined a fine tenor voice for effects that brought down the house. He never could resist the high note of his own resentments: "Most overrated: T. S. Eliot, *all* of him, verse and prose; the academy, or clerisy, needed him as their defense against their own anxieties of uselessness. His neo-Christianity became their mast, hiding their sense of being forlorn and misplaced. His verse is (mostly) weak; his prose is wholly tendentious."[11] It was convenient for Bloom to pretend that the old academy was a form of Christian clerisy, when by and large its pedigree was (in Eliot's lament) Arnoldian. What Bloom really had in mind was a strategy born of the Cold War: a purge that exaggerated the influence of Christian orthodoxy in order to expunge all traces of it from the halls of liberal learning. His criticism typically draws on (and grossly distorts) the Blakean-Paterian-Yeatsian concept of rival genealogies in English poetry: "One line, . . . the central one, is Protestant, radical, and Miltonic-romantic; the other is Catholic, conservative, and by its claims, classical." Bloom then transfers this oppositional structure to the mind of Eliot. This "conflict," he writes, "runs all through the criticism of T. S. Eliot, in many concealments, and it accounts finally for *all* of Eliot's judgments on English poetry." The familiar calumny is that Eliot was led by false consciousness and ideology. But Bloom piles mania on mania, like a crazed titan storming the Olympus of his delusions, hunting some figment of Eliot on his dark throne. Amid the debris of the palace, Bloom crowns himself king by denying that modernism happened. It was, he declares, reheated ersatz romanticism: "Modernism in literature has not passed; rather, it has been exposed as never having been there."[12] Now that's what I call confidence. And if it was inconveniently true that Eliot upheld Arnold's "judgment of the Romantic Generation," that "the English poetry of the first quarter of this century, with plenty of energy, plenty of creative force, did not know enough,"[13] and if it was inconveniently

11. Bloom, quoted by Hilton Kramer, and requoted by Gregory S. Jay, *T. S. Eliot and the Poetics of Literary History,* 69n5.
12. Harold Bloom, *Poetics of Influence: New and Selected Criticism,* 8, 105–6.
13. Arnold, quoted in Eliot, *Sacred Wood,* xii.

true that Arnold was in fact Protestant and liberal, the solution to the problem was obvious. It was to ignore Arnold as well.

Like Vendler, Bloom adopted the handsome strategy of putting his elders on the couch. This move, of shining a Freudian moonbeam into the tortured psyche of the neo-Christians (Bloom targeted a handful of New Critics who offended him at Yale, where he studied poetry in the 1950s), has something faintly ludicrous about it, since the conclusion (the patient is mad) is a prelude to the diagnosis. And why "neo-?" Because it is especially hurtful to label a teacher spiritually inauthentic. Bloom insinuates that Christianity is dead to thinking people, and that art is a truer form of religion. He does not engage his enemies with "a method of carrying on study and debate." No, he cracks open their hoary heads.

Bloom explains himself in *T. S. Eliot,* a collection of essays in his Chelsea House series. In his introduction, he is sensitive to several pressures: his growing authority; Eliot's evident staying power; and the fact that French-inspired theorists were leading not only Eliot to the academic guillotine but Shelley and Stevens also. Bloom's autobiographical instincts prevail, however, and with little ado he unburdens himself:

> To speak out of even narrower personal experience, anyone adopting the profession of teaching literature in the early nineteen fifties entered a discipline virtually enslaved not only by Eliot's insights but by the entire span of his preferences and prejudices. If one's cultural position was Jewish, Liberal and Romantic, one was likely to start out with a certain lack of affection for Eliot's predominance, however much (against the will) the subtle force of the poetry was felt. If a young critic particularly loved Shelley, Milton, Emerson, Pater, and if the same critic did not believe that Blake was a naive and eccentric genius, then regard for Eliot seemed unnecessary. Whatever he actually represented, a neochristian and neoclassical Academy had exalted him, by merit raised, to what was pragmatically rather a bad eminence.[14]

The motif of being "enslaved" and then liberated in an exodus from the 1950s connects Bloom and Vendler to the progressive liberal narrative of the 1960s. Casting the "neochristian" Eliot as Pharaoh, Bloom

14. Harold Bloom, introduction to *T. S. Eliot: Modern Critical Views,* 1.

casts himself as a neo-Moses writing a neo-Torah in the desert of the New Criticism. He allows that Eliot had some talent (another book on Eliot would otherwise be superfluous), and then rises to a gloating comparison of Eliot to the devil (Milton's "Satan exalted sat, by merit raised / To that bad eminence"). What Blake said about Milton, Bloom implies about Eliot: "he was . . . of the Devil's party without knowing it."[15] It is, for some poor scholars, a bitter irony that literary allusions of this kind are lost on readers whom the Eliot-bashers liberated.

A short space later, our gentle critic embarks upon a higher strain:

> Eliot only recently has ceased to represent the spiritual enemy. His disdain for Freud, his flair for demonstrating the authenticity of Christianity by exhibiting a judicious anti-Semitism, his refined contempt for human sexuality—somehow these did not seem to be the inevitable foundations for contemporary culture. Granted that he refrained from the rhetorical excesses of his ally Ezra Pound; there is nothing in him resembling the Poundian apothegm: "All the jew part of the Bible is black evil." Still, an Academy that found its ideology in Eliot was not a place where one could teach comfortably, or where one could have remained, had the Age of Eliot not begun to wane.[16]

Bloom is unbearably wordy, forever substituting words for deeds. Like his master, Emerson, he conflates words and deeds, and so he assumes the manner of a great man looking back on his century.[17] It is as if Bloom's personal experience had blended, in his mind, with some introduction to the universe, defined in Emersonian terms as "the externalization of the soul."[18] By the time he airs Pound's execrable statement, the transition from the verbal act of criticism to the dramatics of self-revelation is complete. As for the "inevitable foundations for contemporary culture," with these sophisticated Bloom would parlay his modest authority into a voice out of the whirlwind. But certainly the foundations in question require more than words. Every

15. William Blake, *Blake's Poetry and Designs*, 88.

16. Bloom, introduction, 1–2.

17. "Words and deeds are quite indifferent modes of the divine energy. Words are also actions, and actions are a kind of words" (Emerson, *Selected Writings*, 322).

18. Ibid., 325.

word is a deed in the sense that it enacts a moral choice. It is a mature moral act to defer to a hierarchy of goods, to appreciate that high creative works are more valuable to culture than even the best criticism.[19] It is a mature moral act to distinguish fact from fiction. And human nature sings out of past depths, in Homer, in *Beowulf*, in the Gawain poet, to caution us that vain boasting should never be confused with heroic action. The tradition, in this respect, is justly hard on critics.

Self-devotedly ungrateful to Eliot ("regard for Eliot seemed unnecessary"), Bloom magnanimously forgives his own immense debt to the poet.[20] He is similarly ungrateful to the *literary establishment* that awarded him the doctorate. You would think Bloom's situation was dire, that he had been exiled to labor at a poor college in the Bible Belt, but anyone acquainted with the period in question will recognize that he overstates his isolation. After writing the mediocre doctoral thesis that became *Shelley's Mythmaking,* he published his first important study of romanticism, *The Visionary Company* (1961), with Eliot's own publishing house, Faber and Faber. Cleanth Brooks, the doyen of the Yale New Critics, wrote in the 1965 "Retrospective Introduction" to his 1939 book *Modern Poetry and the Tradition:* "Today I should want to lay more stress on the extent to which Eliot, Yeats, and the other modern poets built upon the Romantic tradition and incorporated structural devices that are a part of the general Romantic inheritance."[21] Eliot himself, as he aged, did little to encourage the polarization of romantic and modernist that defined a generation of graduate students. He admired Wordsworth, identified with Coleridge, and quoted Shelley with abandon. There was an attempt at a rapprochement with Milton; in fact Bloom was preceded by several distinguished English critics, C. S. Lewis among them, in his dissent from Eliot's judgments on Milton. Even the notorious Blake essay from *The Sacred Wood,* which places Blake high in the pantheon of nondramatic poets, a step below Dante, avoids the extremism of the early Yeats.

19. "Works . . . of genius fall under no art; heroic minds come under no rule; a University is not a birthplace of poets or immortal authors, of founders of schools, leaders of colonies, or conquerors of nations" (John Henry Newman, *The Idea of a University,* 125).

20. See, for example, Jay, *T. S. Eliot;* Perl, *Skepticism;* and Roger Sharrock, "Eliot's Tone."

21. Cleanth Brooks, *Modern Poetry and the Tradition,* xiv.

Managing to sound downtrodden, Bloom refers to himself as a "Liberal" who "particularly loved" Pater, who likewise turns all criticism into self-portraiture. But it would be foolish to ignore Pater's exquisite gifts: his critical acumen, his historical grasp of language, his mesmerizing cadences and psychological glamour. It is Pater who supplies a kind of slender and beautiful bridge, a crumbling remnant of the high culture that Bloom and Vendler accidentally dynamited, even before the ideologues buried the canonical bodies in a mass grave. Do not take these metaphors lightly! Lesser talents quickly learned the trick of demolition, which was simply a matter—to adopt Pater's idiom—of putting *me* first. In the preface to *The Renaissance*, Pater not only withdrew into the haunting quiet of his own mind, he took the Renaissance with him:

> "To see the object as in itself it really is," has been justly said to be the aim of all true criticism whatever; and in aesthetic criticism the first step towards seeing one's object as it really is, is to know one's impression as it really is, to discriminate it, to realize it distinctly. . . . What is this song or picture, this engaging personality presented in life or in book, to *me*? What effect does it really produce on me? . . . How is my nature modified by its presence, and under its influence? The answer to these questions are the original facts with which the aesthetic critic has to do; and as in the study of light, of morals, of number, one must realise such primary data for oneself, or not at all.[22]

It was this passage that inspired Wilde's castration of Arnold, in *The Critic as Artist:* "the primary aim of the critic is to see the object as in itself it really is not."[23] Standards, practices, methods, and so on: all go into twilight, eclipsed by the "primary data" of personality. In effect, Pater's rebellion against Arnold (whom he quotes) reiterates the psychologizing, personalizing effect that Chesterton traced to Luther. The same effect is evident in Bloom. In all three cases, traditional loves and loyalties bow to the subjective glories of the self. The glories are all or nothing, an expression of personal warfare against (in Bloom's words) "the spiritual enemy."

22. Pater, *Works,* 1:viii.
23. Wilde, *Complete Works,* 1030.

There has been an effort to recover Eliot by American critics of the pragmatist school. The pragmatists, to their credit, have kept Eliot in play. But I insist on an unpopular point, namely, that the pragmatist revival has ended badly. The point is not lacking in irony, since the pragmatist himself insists the proof is in the pudding. Certainly pragmatism has not stopped the curriculum from going down the drain.

The notion that pragmatism could invigorate the discipline of English was defended with considerable intelligence and condescension by *Raritan* editor and Emersonian critic Richard Poirier. Poirier argues that Emerson strongly influenced Eliot, although his "potential Emersonianism gives way to the urgency of his personal need for order and, ultimately, for the God of Anglo-Catholicism." This is fair enough. At his most Emersonian, Eliot writes: "To be free we must be stripped, like the sea-god Glaucus, of any number of incrustations of education and frequentation; we must divest ourselves even of our ancestors. But to undertake this stripping of acquired ideas, we must make one assumption: that of the individuality of each human being; we must, in fact, believe in the soul." Emerson said much the same thing in "Self-Reliance," only he took aim at the dogmatic core: "This one fact the world hates; that the soul *becomes;* for that forever degrades the past, turns all riches to poverty, all reputation to shame, confounds the saint with the rogue, shoves Jesus and Judas equally aside." Poirier marches Emerson into poststructuralist territory in order to deny the soul itself, which is "not to be imagined as an entity; it is more nearly a function and yet no determination is made as to when the function occurs or from where it emanates." In effect, Poirier joins Emerson with Heisenberg, to herald the quantum mechanics of fate: "The soul has no determinable there or then, no here or now; rather, as [Emerson's] italics insist, it only *'becomes,'* only promises to make its presence known." It "is like James's will to believe." It "hints at Stevens's 'supreme fiction.'" "In any case . . . the soul always awaits us."[24] Until we are dead, apparently. And until that great day dawns, my dear Theophilus, it is unlikely that the metaphor of quantum mechanics will do much to illuminate truth, goodness, or beauty. We might just as well play dice with dead men's bones.

24. Richard Poirier, *Poetry and Pragmatism,* 21–22; T. S. Eliot, "Notes on the Way," 89; Emerson, *Selected Writings,* 158; Poirier, *Poetry,* 23–24, 24.

Some eminent pragmatists, Richard Rorty among them, have remarked that liberalism can freeload on Christian ethics.[25] In a similar fashion, aesthetes have enjoyed the power of certain verbal combinations or associative patterns from the English literary tradition. This authorial resource or reserve is the mainstay of Poirier's pragmatists, who "make any idea . . . into their own . . . by troping or inflecting or giving a new voice to the idea, by reshaping it, to a degree that makes any expression of gratitude to a previous text wholly unnecessary."[26] By contrast, I think of Dante's filial joy at the apparition of Virgil, in the first Canto of the *Commedia,* as a model of literary gratitude. There is likewise the ending of Chaucer's *Troilus and Criseide:*

> But litel book, no makyng thow n'envie,
> But subgit be to alle poesye;
> And kis the steppes, where as thow seest pace
> Virgile, Ovide, Omer, Lucan and Stace.[27]

It is this type of courteous gesture that Poirier disdains; ingratitude is evidently the hallmark of a certain well-fed generation. But the tradition itself stands on metaphysical foundations or "steppes" that pragmatism is helpless to supply. Either there is permanence in literature, however mysterious its ground, or there is no sense in talking about a tradition, something we hand down for the sake of the human good, which joins us in community. Poirier neglects this, much as he neglects the fact that almost all his privileged forebears, Emerson, Thoreau, Whitman, Dickinson, James, Dewey, are rooted in Protestant Christianity. What an astonishing thing for a critic to overlook.

Richard Shusterman offers a more compelling approach to the pragmatist legacy. In *T. S. Eliot and the Philosophy of Criticism,* Shusterman

---

25. See Richard Rorty, "Postmodern Bourgeois Liberalism." For a Catholic response to these matters, see George Weigel, "Catholicism and Democracy." Weigel's insights into late-twentieth-century democratic politics have lost none of their piquancy: "There was a new specter haunting, not just Europe, but the democratic world as a whole: it was the specter of Weimar Germany, a splendid edifice of finely calibrated democratic institutions built on wholly insufficient moral-cultural foundations" (ibid., 49).

26. Poirier, *Poetry,* 19–20.

27. Geoffrey Chaucer, *The Riverside Chaucer,* 584.

makes Eliot a pragmatist through the likeness between Eliot's "tradition" and Hans-Georg Gadamer's "linguistic community." Shusterman
then suggests that pragmatism can wisely escape the horns of our current critical dilemma:

> Eliot apparently concluded that the only way to stop [the] damag-
> ing pendulum swings of [hedonistic impressionism and joyless
> scholarship] is to insist emphatically that enjoyment and under-
> standing are not essentially opposed but ultimately are inseparable
> features of the activity of reading. This is precisely what he urged
> in "The Frontiers of Criticism," where his more specific goal was to
> rescue criticism from the professional scientism of the university
> scholar by legitimating the personal and the pleasurable in our crit-
> ical response. In this, of course, he anticipates Barthes and other con-
> temporary hedonists, though with characteristic prudence he avoids
> their extremism. Eliot realized that the issues in criticism (and else-
> where) do not admit such facile one-sided resolution; that (as Wilde
> said) the truth is rarely plain and never simple; that the right way
> of right reason or *phronesis* is a difficult interpretive mediation of
> complexities, including those of changing circumstances.[28]

I am afraid that Shusterman proposes a false stability. It may be said
to rest on the forgetting of arguments presented most memorably by
Chesterton—arguments that Eliot took to heart. If we restore the miss-
ing pieces, we find that "professional scientism" is the work of instrumental reason, reason denuded of human value, reason in the Void. The
"contemporary hedonists" are the descendants of Pater. And with the
scientists and the hedonists at loggerheads, thought and feeling are
divorced. Chesterton's basic premise, where he most differs from
Arnold and Shusterman, is that religion is what enables us to relate
thought to feeling. The Christian will feel the weight of Chesterton's
argument, that where "right reason or *phronesis*" is concerned, the
Apostles' Creed is virtually indispensable. The non-Christian might
at least address the strength of Chesterton's observations about the crisis of reason and nature (we have addressed Chesterton's critique of
pragmatism in Chapter 2). Again, one thinks of Rorty's living off the
Christian moral deposit, because the contemporary pragmatist can

---

28. Richard Shusterman, *T. S. Eliot and the Philosophy of Criticism*, 221.

have no universal right reason *(recta ratio)* without premises that precede his epistemology. Chesterton anticipated Rorty's freeloading in 1929: "the modern world, with its modern movements, is living on its Catholic capital. It is using, and using up, the truths that remain to it out of the old treasury of Christendom; including, of course, many truths known to pagan antiquity but crystallized in Christendom. . . . It is not starting fresh things that it can really carry on far into the future."[29] Shusterman's effort is admirable in itself, but it stands on a consensus of convenience that has hurt our culture: the consensus that the religious background can be and maybe should be neglected.

To conclude this examination of critical collapse, I want to underscore the religious question. How did liberal humanism deliver criticism and literature into the weak hands of a New Age clerisy? Vestiges of reason and the natural order survived as long as the canon and scholarly norms prevailed. What was left of liberal humanism kept out chaos for a time, like a natural boundary protecting the community from disaster. Poststructuralist American pragmatism could not stop the damage; its Emersonian and gnostic weather only increased the rate of erosion. As the heretical element grew stronger, the boundary wore away and a new horizon presented itself.

Vendler's 1995 book *Soul Says: On Recent Poetry* and Bloom's tome of 2002, *Genius: A Mosaic of One Hundred Creative Minds,* are prime examples of gnostic aestheticism. What joins the two books is their essentially Emersonian creed of gnostic poetics: "the oldest and best aspects of the self are seen as not being part of nature." For Bloom, "Gnosticism has been indistinguishable from imaginary genius . . . it is pragmatically *the religion of literature.*" Here in fact we uncover the truth of Bloom's splitting the tradition into Catholic and Protestant authors: it is really a split between Christians and gnostics. Vendler proceeds from a dogmatic assertion: "Selves come with a history: souls are independent of time and space."[30] If poetry must do without history, that rules out Homer, Virgil, Dante, the *Beowulf* poet, Chaucer, the Gawain poet, Spenser, Shakespeare, Dryden, Johnson, Wordsworth, Tennyson, Browning, Whitman, C. Rossetti, Dickinson,

29. Chesterton, *Collected Works,* 3:147.

30. Harold Bloom, *Genius: A Mosaic of One Hundred Creative Minds,* xviii; Helen Vendler, *Soul Says: On Recent Poetry,* 5.

Hardy, Frost, Eliot, Marianne Moore, Auden, and Wilbur, to name a few. I think it rules out even Wallace Stevens, whose best poetry (for example, "The River of Rivers in Connecticut") is certainly not "independent of time and space." Where, one asks, are these critics coming from? A cynic might say their behavior is predictable. Having been well rewarded for their anti-Christian posture over the years, they have learned to express that position in what is heretically its purest form. Freed from the tradition of the great poet-critics from Dryden to Eliot, poetry according to Bloom and Vendler speaks for the soul's liberation from human nature and from God, the soul's discovery of its supremacy to the created order.

In a theft that would make even strong poets blush, Bloom seizes Saint Anselm's ontological proof of God's existence: "Shakespeare, like his Hamlet, exceeds us in consciousness, goes beyond the highest order of consciousness that we are capable of knowing without him." I agree that Shakespeare towers over his critics (except Bloom, over whom he *kneels*), but the game of rivaling God was not one our God-haunted playwright cared to play.[31] His morality was too close to natural law; his imagination too close to his sense of grace; his wit too close to the Christian paradox of the *felix culpa,* or happy fall. In sympathy with the created order, Shakespeare is spiritually akin to Chesterton: "The artist loves his limitations: they constitute the *thing* he is doing." Disregard for the "Three Unities" does not negate this spiritual kinship. The very word *thing* is one of Shakespeare's favorites: "How poor

---

31. Bloom, *Genius,* 12. I do not insist on Shakespeare's Christianity; plainly, though, it is not Christian dogmatists who threaten Shakespeare. The following passage is radically destructive of religious, theological, and philosophical avenues to the past: "Though on occasion he depicts ghosts, demons, and other supernatural figures, the universe Shakespeare conjures up seems resolutely human-centered and secular: the torments and joys that most deeply matter are found in this world, not the next" (Stephen Greenblatt, ed., *The Norton Anthology of English Literature,* 496). The idea of a "secular" universe being "resolutely human-centered" is a parochialism that, if it had real weight, would render Christianity culturally superfluous, both to Shakespeare and to us. In reality, the presence of "ghosts, demons, and other supernatural figures" is of relatively minor importance compared to the "resolutely human-centered" impact of Christianity. You would think that the editor of the *Norton Anthology* would have better sense than to write like a schoolboy trying to please his anti-Christian headmaster.

a thing is man . . ."; an "excellent thing in woman." Virgil similarly milks the pathetic effects of *res.* In conflict with the created order, the gnostic has no affection for things, for he thinks of time and space as a prison.[32] "Shakespearean consciousness," writes Bloom (echoing Pater), "transmutes matter into imagination."[33] Why should Bloom violently and recklessly convert Shakespeare from a lover of God-sent miracles to a romantic gnostic who lords it over creation? Because that is what Shakespeare means to *him.* It is his "religion."

Does it follow that "we are still in Arnold's period?" The problem, of course, is that there is scarcely a "we" to discuss. By way of Chesterton, Eliot was able to connect Arnoldian liberal humanism to the spiritual decay of the academy. But by now, the decadence has virtually run its course and can no longer feed off literary studies. The cult of art is dying, Egypt, dying. Leaders of a lost cause, Bloom and Vendler may owe something of their literary faith to Arnold, but they denied what is most lasting in his thought: his sense of tradition, his true pragmatism, his appeal to reason and nature. The future in turn has already denied them; no wonder they are indignant. Bloom had it wrong: gnosticism is not "the religion of literature." Unlike the great books, it is parasitical on orthodoxy and possibly always has been.[34]

32. Chesterton, *Collected Works,* 1:244. To quote Johnson's *Preface to Shakespeare:* "As nothing is essential to the fable but unity of action, and as the unities of time and place arise evidently from false assumptions, and, by circumscribing the extent of the drama, lessen its variety, I cannot think it much to be lamented that they were not known by him, or not observed" (Samuel Johnson, *Selected Poetry and Prose,* 313). See also the classic work by Hans Jonas, *The Gnostic Religion: The Message of the Alien God and the Beginnings of Christianity,* 51–54.

33. Bloom, *Genius,* 12. For Pater, see note 4 of Chapter 3.

34. See Alastair H. B. Longman, *Gnostic Truth and Christian Heresy: A Study in the History of Gnosticism;* and Simone Pétrement, *A Separate God.*

Part IV

THE RADICAL MIDDLE

7

Enter Reason and Nature

In his 1998 encyclical *Fides et Ratio, On the Relationship between Faith and Reason,* John Paul II urges a theological return to philosophy. The argument is scholarly and clear, its pace measured and confident. But the learned author does not want to dominate the philosophical heights. His purpose is to invite others to share them, and in this respect his effort breathes the ecumenical air of the Second Vatican Council. Back in the Edwardian decade, when Chesterton was writing *Heretics* and *Orthodoxy,* there occurred what church historians call the modernist crisis, when Pius X collided with the twentieth century by denouncing post-Thomistic theology.[1] For Catholic modernists, the old theology seemed frozen in time, while their love of truth drew them to new methods issuing from the Enlightenment, especially in the field of history. A century later, there are noted philosophers for whom Karol Wojtyla is more up-to-date than Jacques Derrida.

According to John Paul II, the main contemporary schools of philosophy are neglecting "the radical question of the truth about personal existence, about being and about God." The "hope," he writes, "that philosophy might be able to provide definite answers to these questions has dwindled." In his rejection of "'philosophical pride,' which seeks to present its own partial and imperfect view as the complete reading of all reality," he conveys a fresh commitment on the Church's part toward philosophical diversity. As a Christian humanist,

---

1. For rival views of the modernist crisis, see Johnson, *History of Christianity,* 471–76; and Aidan Nichols, O.P., *The Shape of Catholic Theology: An Introduction to Its Sources, Principles, and History,* 331–34. For Eliot and theological modernism, see Donald J. Childs, *T. S. Eliot: Mystic, Son, and Lover.*

he defends both the project of philosophy and the work of independent philosophers. He holds that "every philosophical system, while it should always be respected in its wholeness, without any instrumentalization, must still recognize the primacy of philosophical enquiry, from which it stems and which it ought loyally to serve." Yet this solution, which seems the very soul of humanistic reasonableness, remains painfully open to criticism. John Paul, it can be argued, is a philosopher in the old sense, a metaphysician who assumes a philosophical "core" in "right reason or, as the ancients called it, orth(o-)s logos, recta ratio."[2] It can be argued that philosophy in the old sense is obsolete: many professional philosophers have in fact given up on systematic philosophy, metaphysics, and the philosophical tradition.

From the Church's historical perspective, this intellectual falling off has much to do with Kant. John Paul refers to the First Vatican Council, which upheld the supernatural character of Revelation against the Kantian move of bracketing all knowledge beyond the seemingly natural limits of understanding.[3] In his defense of rational theology, which Kant would effectively annihilate, John Paul seeks to rescue reality itself from destruction. The situation confronting him can be characterized as follows. Absent Revelation, Kant showed that pure reason lacks stability. Luther had called reason a whore, and Kant in a sense proved him right. He could do whatever he wanted with pure reason: prove that the world had a beginning in time, or prove it had no beginning; prove that freedom exists, or prove there is no freedom. In effect, Kant achieved an existential trade-off in the life of reason. He was morally a rationalist, but in order to make his rational system work, he partitioned off reality. His realism was minimal. He gave the world transcendental idealism in order to save the phenomena that we ordinarily observe. This is the basis for Kant's famous metaphor of the Copernican revolution: as the heavens appear to revolve around the observer, so in metaphysics the temporal, spatial, and causal order is likewise a function of the perceiving mind. But transcendental idealism has had a consequence that Kant did not intend: it has concealed reality behind an ever-thickening wall of appearances, constructs, and interpretations.

2. John Paul II, *Fides et Ratio,* sec. 5, sec. 4.
3. Ibid., sec. 8.

John Paul's defense of reason finds an unlikely ally in Thomas Nagel, a leading moral and political theorist. Both Wojtyla and Nagel judge our intellectual life to be unravelling. One laments theologians who, "through a lack of critical competence, allow themselves to be swayed uncritically by assertions that have become part of current parlance and culture but which are poorly grounded in reason."[4] The other laments "the already extreme intellectual laziness of contemporary culture and the collapse of serious argument throughout the lower reaches of the humanities." For Nagel, an atheist who acknowledges theism as a live option, reason is the indispensable ally of any good society. By "reason," he refers to a "court of appeal" with "universal authority."[5] This is "Reason" with a capital *R:* the abstract entity of humanistic faith.

Nagel challenges transcendental idealism in ways that satisfy the realist impulse behind the *adaequatio rei et intellectus* (the adequation of thing and mind), formulated by Aquinas and Bonaventure, minimized by Kant, dismissed by William James, and reaffirmed by John Paul as "proper to faith." Discussing why realism is unpopular, Nagel remarks, "The thought that the relation between mind and world is something fundamental makes many people in this day and age nervous. I believe this is one manifestation of a fear of religion which has large and often pernicious consequences for modern intellectual life." In his response to Kant, he argues, "we are entitled to employ the forms of reasoning which the theory purports to disqualify as ways of determining what the world is really like." Kant proposed that the order we appear to find in nature is an interface we impose on experience. Nagel contends that by light of reason's procedures of hypothesis, experiment, and plausibility, idealist Kantians must yield to the realist point of view, namely, that "the order we find in our experience is the product of an order that is there independent of our minds."[6] Put simply, it is unacceptable to believe in the periodic table or the gravitational redshift as products of Kant's transcendental deduction.

Nagel holds that evolution did not introduce reason to the cosmos. More specifically, he doubts that evolution could hardwire us for an essentially groundless faith in reason's practical ability to grasp reality.

4. Ibid., sec. 55.
5. Thomas Nagel, *The Last Word,* 6, 3.
6. John Paul II, *Fides et Ratio,* sec. 82; Nagel, *Last Word,* 130, 95.

(If reason were only more persuasive, the argument with post-Kantian idealism might end right there.) What Nagel proposes is a "more general category of *mind*."[7] Reason leads him toward theism: he stops short of belief in God, but reason leaves belief open to him or to anyone. In a chagrined note, he observes the strong teleological implications of his argument, but he remains a philosopher to the bitter end.

David Tracy is a Catholic theologian who does not sound at all like the pope. He is best known for his work *The Analogical Imagination,* in which he commits himself to the antirealist statement, "We understand one another, if at all, through analogy." This new dogmatism is rooted in the hermeneutic tradition of Schleiermacher, Dilthey, and Heidegger, all of whom would make interpretation our fundamental way of knowing the world. It is difficult, not to say impossible, for some of us to countenance that Catholic theology has anything to do with this approach. If the essence of Christianity is just another story about the truth, and not the truth itself, then it must just compete as best it can with Buddhist stories or (if you like) Aryan myths of racial supremacy. Its grip on the affections weakens, and it loses its evangelical character. Tracy's theological imperative is "the necessity of radical theological negations to constitute all Christian theological language."[8] The statement is not far removed from *Waiting for Godot.* It shows, I think, an aesthetic-historicist approach to theology. And though the principle of negative (or apophatic) theology is permanent, Tracy radicalizes it far more than the tradition can accommodate. An orthodox Christian must by definition believe that the Incarnation puts certain stories, and the theological language of those stories, beyond the reach of "radical . . . negations." That is why Chesterton founded the argument of *Orthodoxy* on the Apostles' Creed. Along the same lines, Anglican theologian N. T. Wright argues that Christianity stands or falls by its historical record. Basic elements of the Gospel, such as Saint Paul's list of witnesses who saw the risen Christ, are as true (or false) as they ever were.[9] When Paul tells the church at Corinth, "If Christ has not been raised, your faith is futile"

7. Nagel, *Last Word,* 140.

8. David Tracy, *The Analogical Imagination: Christian Theology and the Culture of Pluralism,* 454, 415.

9. See, for example, N. T. Wright, *The Resurrection of the Son of God,* 382.

(1 Cor. 15:17 *NRSV*), he does not mean "raised" analogically, or metaphorically, or symbolically. In fact, at Corinth, he encountered sophisticated Christians for whom Jesus was no more than a myth.[10]

Differing from Tracy does not entail neglecting the historical dimension of human thought. History sheds significant light on many things, not least of all the Lord's Prayer and Paul's account of the Last Supper. But what is worse than neglecting historicism is usurping the past and calling it historicism. Tracy bases his position on Hegel: "the fact that reason has a history is a problem for reason." Here the walls in the temple of thought start to shake. But the best answer may be to recognize that those walls rest on foundations that antedate the earth. I argue that the limits of reason should not impoverish reason, and that the history of reason should not impoverish history. The *Zeitgeist,* which Arnold thought was "sapping the proof from miracles," cannot explain the relation between a Romanized Jew like Josephus and a member of the Sanhedrin, or the radically divergent responses to Christ from Jew and Greek. The Word was made flesh, and that is why the story of the Incarnation was and is available to mankind. But the historical imagination begins, as Shakespeare suggests, with "humble patience" and prayer.[11]

The finer points of orthodoxy constitute a burning ground that we must tread with care. Eliot insightfully remarks, "we hardly expect every theologian to be orthodox in every particular, for it is not the sum of theologians, but the Church itself, in which orthodoxy resides." Theology, as John Paul makes clear, is written and read in the light of history. In *Fides et Ratio,* he notes that early "Christian thinkers were critical in adopting philosophical thought." "Before Origen," he writes, "the name 'theology' itself, together with the idea of theology as a rational discourse about God, had been tied to Greek origins."[12] And he goes on to quote Tertullian's famous riposte, "What does Athens have in common with Jerusalem? The Academy with the Church?" A superb reasoner, Tertullian nonetheless repressed the rationalist, Greek strain in Christianity in favor of a nonhierarchical Church

---

10. See Johnson, *History of Christianity,* 45.

11. David Tracy, *Dialogue with the Other: The Inter-Religious Dialogue,* 45; Arnold, *Complete Prose Works,* 6:246; Shakespeare, prologue to *Henry V.*

12. Eliot, *After Strange Gods,* 34; John Paul II, *Fides et Ratio,* sec. 39.

of the Spirit. He was a brilliant absolutist, whom a modern Catholic may admire without adulation. In fact, he eventually embraced heresy and joined the Montanists, but his contribution to the Church, as the first great Latin theologian, made him indispensable to the orthodox. In light of such complex spiritual issues, John Paul outlines a continuing (and unfinished) dialectic in the Church's long tradition, where Tertullian's paradoxical thesis, "credo quia absurdum est" ("I believe because it is absurd"), runs counter to Anselm's more progressive faith, "credo ut intellegam" ("I believe in order to understand"), and its equally optimistic inversion, "intellego ut credam" ("I understand in order to believe"), both of which furnish *Fides et Ratio* with chapter headings. Like Eliot's "tongues of flame," the diverse voices of these saints and sages are folded into a mystical order that transcends them.

Granted, then, that our understanding of the relation between reason and God is not angelic, the issue at hand is whether Tracy's theology has any constructive orthodox features, or whether it is primarily destructive in its effects (though not in its intentions). In 1989, Tracy delivered a series of lectures at the University of Louvain, published in 1991 under the title *Dialogue with the Other: The Inter-Religious Dialogue.* The Louvain lectures begin ominously with an attack upon the Eurocentric character of Christian theology. The Eurocentric character of hermeneutics attracts no comment. Tracy's method of approach is to call into question "the Enlightenment notion of rationality," which is how Tracy refers to universal reason.[13] Despite the fact that Enlightenment philosophy disowned faith, I do not see how this conception of reason, per se, differs from that of Wojtyla or Nagel. For all intents and purposes, it is Reason with a capital *R.* Tracy discusses the limits of rationality in a lecture called "Rethinking William James," from which I quote:

> Several recent Western philosophical discussions of reason itself are helpful for fighting [the] scientific temptation [of demanding a "set of cognitive criteria (under rubrics, for example, like strict verification and strict falsification)"]. In an intellectual situation where even philosophers of natural science . . . have challenged earlier reigning paradigms of scientism and "rationality," many (to be sure, not all) in the philosophical community have far more flexible notions of

13. Tracy, *Dialogue with the Other,* 1.

"truth" and "reason" than was the case in the heyday of positivism. Science itself is now acknowledged as a hermeneutic enterprise. . . . Of course, there is no *de facto* consensus among contemporary philosophers on what rational consensus in principle is. This, for the purposes of interreligious dialogue, is not necessarily unfortunate. If philosophers like [Richard] Bernstein show a genuinely rational way to recover the classical resources of reason (e.g. Aristotelian *phronesis* and Peirce's "community of inquiry") then, minimally, the discussion of "reason and religion" should be freed from what Bernstein nicely labels "objectivism" and "relativism."[14]

It is regrettable that William James should get dragged into this, William who groused to his brother Henry while finishing the *Principles of Psychology:* "I have to forge every sentence in the teeth of irreducible and stubborn facts."[15] What stands out in Tracy's own prose (making it appear much more like Henry's than like William's) is the heavy use of quotation marks: all this grasping and sterilizing is a symptom of language in decline. Tracy does not use his terms for purposes of definition; instead, he uses them, like Shakespeare's Lavinia entering with her hands cut off, to gesture at a wide and conflicting range of interpretive possibilities. His innocent remark that "Science itself is now acknowledged as a hermeneutic enterprise" might be penned by Alan Sokal.[16]

Tracy's "radical theological negations" are prophetically answered by Newman, who defends traditional theology in the liberal arts. "Physical Science itself," Newman warns, "will ultimately be the loser by . . . ill treatment of Theology."[17] Newman's argument regarding Newton (as the paladin of science) fits just as well with Einstein:

> The Newtonian philosophy requires the admission of certain metaphysical postulates . . . that there is such a thing as matter, that our senses are trustworthy, that there is a logic of induction, and so on.

---

14. Ibid., 45.

15. William James, quoted in Alfred North Whitehead, *Science and the Modern World,* 3.

16. Sokal has exposed shameless scientific fraud among the French crowd whose names Tracy invokes like a litany of academic saints. See Sokal and Bricmont, *Fashionable Nonsense.*

17. Newman, *Idea,* 157.

> Now to Newton metaphysicians grant all that he asks; but if so be, they may not prove equally accommodating to another who asks something else, and then all his most logical conclusions in the science of physics would remain hopelessly on the stocks, though finished, and never could be launched into the sphere of fact.[18]

The author of *The Idea of a University*, probably the most enduring work on liberal education, teaches that the major disciplines must stand together or fall together. Logic and science cannot ignore the corruption of theology, for they benefit from the metaphysical unity that theology protects. This wholeness is intrinsic to Einstein, whose theories of relativity would collapse if the universe was thoroughly relativistic and disunited. In the most practical sense, the balkanization of the cosmos would destroy the Socratic project of science and drain the resources of our comprehension, including intellectual stamina and dialogue.

I can respect Tracy's fear of Roman Catholic domination, though Rome has also proved capable of self-criticism and dialogue. I agree that the historical character of reason and theology cannot and should not be ignored. The real issue is conserving the grounds for true progress. And the problem is that Tracy's corrective measures leave those grounds exposed to the insidious consumer ideology that he rightly deplores. When he disowns hierarchical reasoning, he is not serving the good but silencing it. Without a realist basis, reason becomes a slave to manic consumerism, to intellectual hatred, to artificial needs and undisciplined desires. But given a realist basis, reason must operate hierarchically:

> the outermost framework of all thoughts must be a conception of what is objectively the case—what is the case without subjective or relative qualification. [Further], the task of bringing our thoughts within such a framework involves a reliance on some types of thought to regulate and constrain others, which identify general reasons and thereby advance objectivity. This introduces a hierarchy in which reason provides regulative methods and principles, and perception and intuition provide reason with initial material to work on.[19]

18. Ibid., 44.
19. Nagel, *Last Word*, 16.

By training their natural intellect on reality, some men and women grasp the requisite "methods and principles." Their power is not the subordination of others, not "power" hypostatized in the Foucauldian fashion, but thought itself. And thought turns on certain mechanics we cannot escape, for we rely on them in any attempt to rethink them. Any argument (in any era) that lacks a rational structure will not conduce well to dialogue or translation. If the logical rules of contraposition and inference do not obtain, we are left with so much goo.

Let me say what I am not attempting to do. I am not arguing that reason can substitute for wisdom or prove that God is real. Reason emerges from depths it cannot fathom. History has ruled against the logical positivists, who thought scientific language could yield a full account of true and not true. Their bizarrely constructed reality was surreal. Lacking an understanding of how their analyses worked, they were too much like the scientist whose sesquipedalian formula proves he does not exist.

I am not presenting a rational vindication of morality. Kant tried to do so. Even if we do not agree with Nietzsche that the project was a sham, a fabric of rationalizations woven to conceal the will to power, yet we can say in all fairness that Kant's categorical imperative is empty formalism unless culture supplies the individual with moral choices or maxims. Kant was more indebted to his native Lutheranism than he knew; he is the prototype of the modern moral philosopher who underestimates the importance of Christianity.

I have argued only that reason is indispensable to the good life. It mediates between nature and culture; it also mediates between disciplines. It guides the natural virtues. It is the keystone of our theological arch. It may be said to form a trellis for the imagination. I risk this last figure of speech to allow for the nonrational element in the germ and fruit of the higher imagination, to suggest that reason serves as a trellis or structure of support for the grapes.

But this humanistic perspective has powerful and intelligent critics, some of them within the Church. In *The City of God,* Saint Augustine discredited the Roman historian Sallust for saying that "'equity and virtue prevailed among the Romans not more by force of laws than of nature.'" Augustine replied with disdainful urbanity: "I presume it is to this inborn equity and goodness of disposition we are to ascribe the rape of the Sabine women. What, indeed, could be more equitable and virtuous, than to carry off by force, as each man was fit, and without their parents' consent, girls who were strangers and guests, and who had been decoyed and entrapped by the pretence of a spectacle!"[20] Augustine was the first Christian to sack Rome; his severity is mitigated only by the fact that *The City of God* is a work of apologetics, written to defend the faith against the Gibbonesque charge of corrupting the empire. With broad strokes, he attributes the political and military success of the Romans to the hard work and foresight of a few staunch early republicans; otherwise all was corruption or, at best, virtue made to serve honor, glory, and power. A partial exception is made for Virgil, whom Augustine believed had foretold the birth of Christ.[21] But while Augustine begins *The City of God* with two biblical quotations followed by one from the *Aeneid* ("Show pity to the humbled soul, / And crush the sons of pride") that breathes the righteous spirit of the biblical references, yet he does not attribute this righteousness to the Romans themselves.[22] In the earlier *Confessions,* the same pattern holds of ambivalent borrowing from Roman culture. Augustine denounces the *Aeneid* ("a most enchanting dream, futile though it was"),[23] while echoing the narrative of Aeneas, an allusive effect not lost on Eliot. A magnificent author, thinker, and stylist, Augustine used his episcopal chair to quash the humanistic tradition of ancient Rome. For theological and personal reasons, he rigged the court of history and denied the Romans a fair hearing.

If we accept the doctrine of Original Sin, a question of emphasis arises. To what extent are our wills capable of good? Chesterton saw profound conflict between the Aristotelian tradition, which runs through the moral theology of Aquinas, and the Augustinian tradition, which runs through the moral theology of Luther. The traditions agree that nature is good in itself. One tradition teaches the potential for good in fallen human nature, the other teaches the potential for evil in fallen human nature. Chesterton summarized Luther's view as follows: "Man could say nothing to God, nothing from God, nothing about God, except an almost inarticulate cry for mercy and for the

20. Augustine, *The City of God,* 55.

21. Gilbert Highet, *The Classical Tradition: Greek and Roman Influences on Western Literature,* 73.

22. Virgil in the *Aeneid* condemns the rape of the Sabine women, exposing this "lawless" act on the great shield of the hero.

23. Augustine, *Confessions,* 35.

supernatural help of Christ, in a world where all natural things were useless. Reason was useless. Will was useless." We encounter much the same complex in Beckett, who describes art as the "expression that there is nothing to express, nothing with which to express, nothing from which to express, no power to express, no desire to express, together with the obligation to express."[24] Chesterton, it must be admitted, does not always do justice to the depth and complexity of Augustine or Luther. History vindicates the Reformation, which was needed for modern western democracy to happen. On the other hand, the negative side of the Reformation is clear. Common sense, the common good, and the Church's power to renew itself have all fallen victim to the privatization of religious life.

The leading Catholic remedy for this modern sickness is Thomism. In *Fides et Ratio,* John Paul quotes his predecessor Paul VI:

> The key point and almost the kernel of the solution which, with all the brilliance of his prophetic intuition, [Saint Thomas] gave to the new encounter of faith and reason was a reconciliation between the secularity of the world and the radicality of the Gospel, thus avoiding the unnatural tendency to negate the world and its values while at the same time keeping faith with the supreme and inexorable demands of the supernatural order.[25]

This "solution" is not for everybody. Even so wise and creative a thinker as F. H. Bradley, in building a moral synthesis that includes Luther and Aristotle, could not endorse "a reconciliation between the secularity of the world and the radicality of the Gospel." Bradley (God bless him!) upheld the "eternal glory" of Protestantism. He found that a divided moral consciousness was inevitable.[26] It is, I think, quite possible that the condition described by Bradley is intrinsic to fallen man. The weak version of humanism, which descends from Bradley to Eliot, may be existentially truer than the strong version, which descends from Chesterton and the neo-Thomists. And Bradley must sound virtually Thomistic to a Muslim.

24. Chesterton, *Collected Works,* 2:549; Samuel Beckett and Georges Duthuit, "Three Dialogues," 17.
25. Paul VI, quoted in John Paul II, *Fides et Ratio,* sec. 43.
26. F. H. Bradley, *Ethical Studies,* 322–26.

In his moral philosophy, Saint Thomas is an Aristotelian: we are what we do. Grace "does not abolish nature, but completes it."[27] Grace is not the same as virtue, which can survive if left to its own devices. This dramatic acting out of our moral destiny accords with mimesis in art and with the idea of natural law as a rule of conduct. It links ethics to politics, and it makes for a strong "this-worldly" element in orthodox Christianity. On the other hand, it neglects the hidden places revealed by modern psychology. I will briefly examine how this Thomistic oversight leaves an opening for antihumanism.

The more we privilege modern psychology, the more we will tend to isolate the self from community, and the more we will tend to doubt the connection between moral goodness and the good life. It is therefore unsurprising that virtue ethics has been besieged by psychologists. The most eminent in this class of thinkers are Nietzsche and Freud: a German Lutheran (a pastor's son) and an Austrian Jew. Neither has much use for Aristotle or the classical job of philosophy, the effort to master knowledge. It is true, for example, that Aristotle has no equivalent for unconscious drives, like Nietzsche's will to power or Freud's Oedipus complex. Though no serious scholar would charge that Aristotle rationalizes the mystery of tragedy, nonetheless it can be argued the *Poetics* hesitates before the depths of fatalism and Dionysian power: it can also be argued that our irrational fixation with sex and death amounts to a tragic flaw that can only be understood in light of the good. Freud, who possessed a rare gift for neologisms ("fixation" is Freudian), shared the tragic sense of our erotic and political lives that makes Virgil, as Eliot rightly called him, "the classic of all Europe."[28] But the general influence of Freud is an analytic reduction of the psyche to sexual theater. I give more credit to Nietzsche, whose sensitivity to tragically rich and sublime conflicts between the virtues affords a reach of perception that precedes Freud, goes beyond Virgil, and is alien to Aristotle and Aquinas.

For reasons of health and sanity, we need to conserve a moral foundation in human nature, which is just what Nietzsche and Freud

27. Thomas Aquinas, *Essential Writings of Saint Thomas Aquinas,* 62. See also Etienne Gilson, *The Christian Philosophy of St. Thomas Aquinas,* 259. The tension between Saint Thomas's moral philosophy and his Christianity is a problem well beyond my present resources.

28. T. S. Eliot, *On Poetry and Poets,* 70.

deny.[29] Nietzsche and Freud oppose Aristotle in their common thesis, which we find in Schopenhauer, that the root source of our individual being is a force or will that we placate with metaphysical illusion. Like Schopenhauer, Nietzsche and Freud purport to unmask the humanistic faith in reason and nature. But the humanist can reject what is untrue in their work while acknowledging their disquieting psychological insights. To undertake the civilizing task of humanism, people must believe they are operating on the level of reality. No artist or scientist or teacher will make monumental sacrifices for the Freudian sake of "satisfactions" that "figuratively" "seem 'finer and higher,'" if *seem* is the operative word, and "finer and higher" come dangling at arm's length from quotation marks.[30] If all the world's a scam, then all the world's a scam. Virtue is a conscious, volitional activity, which cannot thrive in the Land of Weasels. So the proof at hand is practical, not conclusive. If civilization is even a practical good (leaving aside whether it is a peak of nature), it follows that what Nietzsche and Freud have to offer is poison, though poison in the right dose can clear and concentrate your mind.

Instead of fighting a hopeless rearguard action, Christian thinkers have learned from modern psychology without bowing down before it. If we study modern psychology in its historical descent, we can begin with Augustine's interior quest for God and continue our journey of inwardness through Descartes and then Locke, with a collateral line running from Augustine to Luther.[31] The Augustinian strain is strong in Eliot, but Eliot was censorious of any psychologist claiming the authority of positivist science. He criticized Freud with the remark, "I can understand, though I do not approve, the naturalistic system of morals based upon biology and analytical psychology (what is valid in these consists largely of things that were always known)." Throughout his career, Eliot studiously avoided Freudian jargon.[32] But one of his

29. For the choice between Aristotle and Nietzsche, see Alasdair MacIntyre, *After Virtue.*

30. Sigmund Freud, *Civilization and Its Discontents,* 28.

31. For the Augustinian strain in modern psychology, see Charles Taylor, *Sources of the Self: The Making of Modern Identity.*

32. Eliot, *Selected Essays,* 432. "The natural waking life of our Ego is a perceiving," in the *Coriolan* sequence, comes, it has been pointed out, by way of Husserl (Eliot, *Collected Poems,* 125).

best dramatic creations, Sir Henry Harcourt-Reilly, is a psychologist in such powerful reaction against Freud as indirectly to compliment the original. Sir Henry tells a patient: "as for your dreams, / You would produce amazing dreams, to oblige me. / I could make you dream any kind of dream I suggest."[33] This jab at the author of *The Interpretation of Dreams* serves to remind us that Eliot was keenly interested in psychological illnesses, and that Sir Henry devotes many fine lines to analyzing them. Like Freud, Frazer, and Picasso, Eliot was fascinated by primitive man, as we see in his reference to the anthropologist Lévy-Bruhl: "the pre-logical mentality persists in civilised man, but becomes available only to or through the poet." Eliot believed that, psychologically, "the poet is *older* than other human beings." The "roots that clutch" go deep; and Eliot's powers of poetic suggestion combine with his dreamlike imagery to reach far back into the mind. But Eliot is reserved where Freud is obtrusive, and it is certainly wiser to admit "feelings too obscure for the authors even to know quite what they were" than to write sheaves of bogus case histories.[34]

There are grounds to suggest that Tolkien, like C. S. Lewis, had a strong intuition of positive evil, verging on dualism.[35] Lewis found evidence for dualism in the New Testament. He recognized the danger of Manichaeanism and, while stopping short of heresy, conceded ambiguity.[36] The same kind of metaphysical problem exists in *The Lord of the Rings,* where the Ring manifests a will of its own. Gandalf describes the Ring to Frodo as an agent in the story: "It was not Gollum . . . but the Ring itself that decided things. The Ring left *him.*" Weirdly beautiful, the Ring alters physically in size, psychologically in weight, and catches the eye when it wants to. Its demonic power clarifies the need for heroic action. What is peculiarly modern in Tolkien's intuition of evil is how he differs from Aquinas with regard to the orthodox Augustinian teaching that positive evil does not exist. He is closer to Kierkegaard, to Nietzsche, and to Yeats, all of whom recognize a creative element in the conflict of psychological drives or, as Nietzsche

33. T. S. Eliot, *The Complete Poems and Plays: 1909–1950,* 348.

34. Eliot, *Use of Poetry,* 141n, 148, 141.

35. I am indebted in this discussion to Shippey, *Road to Middle-earth,* 107–11.

36. See C. S. Lewis, *Mere Christianity,* 46–51.

called them, "*inspiring* spirits."[37] Lothlórien is all the more achingly lovely because it is threatened by powerful evil, and the fate of the Elven Rings is tied to the One. The Lord of the Rings is not, we are reminded, Frodo Baggins. The novel is majestically named after the Enemy.

Like Nietzsche and Yeats, Chesterton put the collision of passions into a creative framework—in his case, Christianity itself, as we have seen in Chapter 2. His historical consciousness was larger than that of Aquinas. Like Nietzsche and Yeats, he pursued emotional truths that are primitive, profound, and elusive. He can also be compared in this respect with Maritain. Chesterton characterizes all the important emotions, like our emotions when we leave flowers for the dead, as "irrational." He characterizes the Christian virtues of faith, hope, and charity as "unreasonable," by which he means "paradoxical." On the subject of modern poetry, Maritain argues that its sources reside in "the preconceptual life of the intellect," and that it "obliges us to consider the intellect both in its secret wellsprings inside the human soul and as functioning in a nonrational (not irrational) or nonlogical way."[38] This hairsplitting between the irrational and the unreasonable and the nonrational can be a distraction. What Chesterton and Maritain have in common is Christian paradox. They seek to ascend through the depths and tensions of psychology toward the highest good: a redemptive God before whom Christian humanism is ultimately awed and silent.

Having seen the modern challenge to philosophy in Nietzsche and Freud, as well as Christian humanism becalmed, or anchored in a nonprogressive if meditative silence, we may be tempted to jump ship and get out of the philosophical game. We can trim our sails to exclude the "democracy of the dead." We can roam the information superhighway, or find some other way to escape all these unappeased spirits, most of all John Paul II, with his daunting battle on two fronts, in philosophy and theology. We can, as a last resort, limit Christianity to the level of solidarity and rights, and never contemplate the source of our freedoms. But to quote Louis Bouyer: "Destitute . . . of a solid theological foundation, lacking a competent philosophy, the devotion

37. Tolkien, *Fellowship of the Ring,* 65; Nietzsche, *Basic Writings,* 203.
38. Chesterton, *Collected Works,* 1:122, 124; Jacques Maritain, *Creative Intuition in Art and Poetry,* 4.

to Christ, as Saviour and God, seems to float on the surface of thought rather than take root therein."[39] Without depth of thought, justice and love become unreal. Our passions are sentimentalized and suppressed. Reality itself is hidden from us and solidarity becomes another means of social control. Literature, benefiting from philosophy and theology, restores thought to feeling. And it is to literature that we now return.

39. Bouyer, *Erasmus and His Times,* 217. I have slightly changed the translation for the sake of clarity.

8

An Imperfect Theory

Arnold was advancing a comprehensive definition in 1879 when he argued that poetry is "a criticism of life." "No phrase," Eliot countered in 1928, "can sound more frigid to anyone who has felt the full surprise and elevation of a new experience in poetry."[1] He expatiated a few years later at Harvard:

> It is in [Arnold's] essay on Wordsworth that occurs his famous definition: "Poetry is at bottom a criticism of life." At bottom: that is a great way down; the bottom is the bottom. At the bottom of the abyss is what few ever see, and what those cannot bear to look at for long; and it is not "a criticism of life." If we mean life as a whole . . . from top to bottom, can anything that we can say of it ultimately, of that awful mystery, be called criticism?[2]

When Eliot turned his Christian back on Arnold, the Augustinian aspect of modernism prevailed. "At the bottom of the abyss" the younger Eliot saw what Kurtz saw: "The horror! the horror!"—more Conrad than Dante, more Schopenhauer than Christianity. His need for grace, when it came, made all other desires seem hollow by comparison. Given the *frisson* of such superb disillusionment (a "new experience," to be sure), and given the sincerity of Eliot's faith (which I do not doubt—I am referring to the temperament of that great poet), it would be superfluous to remark that "criticism" comes from a Greek word meaning "judgment," as in the Last Judgment, a criticism of life if ever there was one. Arnold's approach to literature was oriented to

---

1. Eliot, *Sacred Wood,* ix.
2. Eliot, *Use of Poetry,* 103.

the common reader. It was pitched at a middle-class audience that the modernists instinctively snubbed. It was not a window on "the abyss." Despite his blind spots, Arnold wanted literature to delight and instruct the democratic nations. And if he could not plumb Eliot's mystical depths, yet he avoided the mannerisms of aesthetic unreality that threaten, at times, to lock Eliot within his own period.

There is a hint of modernist conceit or unrepentant aestheticism behind Eliot's apparently straightforward remark: "Poetry is of course not to be defined by its uses." Eliot means that poetry has varying uses over time; subsequently, our definition will be narrow if we define all poetry in terms of our current needs. At Harvard, Eliot's unspoken premise of an absolute that mysteriously governs the field of discourse (for example, "the mind of Europe") lifts him above the battle lines of literary history: "the criticism of no one man and of no one age can be expected to embrace the whole nature of poetry or exhaust all of its uses." More: "every effort to formulate the common element is limited by the limitations of particular men in particular places and at particular times; and these limitations become manifest in the perspective of history."[3] These words are not said to Arnold's detriment. There is, moreover, something admirably modest in the argument: it militates against the Hegelian-Marxist conceit of writing history from the vantage of some triumphal end game. Such hubristic historiography usually falls hardest when judged by later generations. And yet a touch of social or gnostic estrangement marks an activity that is "not to be defined by its uses."

Newman had applied the rhetoric of uselessness against utilitarianism, and Eliot quotes Newman's associate, the "Catholic Whig" historian Lord Acton: "I think our studies ought to be all but purposeless. They want to be pursued with chastity like mathematics."[4] This is an appeal to *theoria*, the leisurely pursuit of knowledge that Aristotle conceived to be intellectual bliss. Leaving aside the fact that Eliot was not an Aristotelian, it is fair to point out that the rose of *theoria* grows in only the finest gardens. Certainly the means to transcend the uses of literature are scarce in modernity. First, with respect to teaching literature, one requires a balance between the independence and the inter-

3. Ibid., 148–49, 134–35.
4. Lord Acton, quoted in Eliot, *Notes,* 85.

connectedness of various disciplines, such as Aristotle achieved through his metaphysic, and such as Newman envisioned through theology; otherwise literature will be usurped by some rival discipline, or corrupted by an alien metaphysic or hostile ideology. Hence it happens today that truth, goodness, and beauty—indispensable criteria for judging literature—are regarded with a power of suspicion worthy of Cerberus. And second, one requires a community with a living tradition. In the continually uprooted world of modernity, science for its own sake, art for its own sake, and study for its own sake require wealth and sanctuary that few lives are privileged to enjoy. And those lives, if they are compassionate, must carry the burden of tragic conflict. Even in Aristotle's day, the joys of *theoria* were rare.

The aesthete's answer to this "usefulness problem" is stated by Wilde, who writes in the preface to *The Picture of Dorian Gray*, "All art is quite useless." Wilde assumes that beauty is all that matters, that goodness and truth are either aspects of beauty or affectations. Eliot of course does not go quite so far. He does not allow poetry to have a universal definition, but he acknowledges that particular uses exist. He resembles Wilde, though, in disconnecting the good of art from moral teleology. Santayana says of Dante: "His art is, in the original Greek sense, an imitation or rehearsal of nature, an anticipation of fate."[5] Despite countless allusions to Dante, Eliot's art, prior to his conversion, was not of this kind. Eliot replaced nature with an order of his own, a fleshless order built out of great books, one of which was the *Divine Comedy*. Priests of art will tend toward this extreme position, slighting the political animal in favor of a gnostic remove from moral life. To dwell alone with beauty, to know her unworldly embrace, the aesthete represses the moral emotions that attach to our physical being. He splits into a disembodied soul and a fallen body. Doing so, he denies his moral nature, much, for instance, as the state of Dorian Gray's soul is concealed along with his portrait. For Wilde, conflict returns through the curious fact that *The Picture of Dorian Gray* ends in moral tragedy. The novel does not adhere to the gnostic dandyism of its preface.

We may wonder if Eliot has justice with him in his quasi-cubist approach to the use of poetry. Is he claiming many perspectives where

---

5. Wilde, *Complete Works,* 17; George Santayana, *Three Philosophical Poets: Lucretius Dante Goethe,* 113.

Arnold gets one? Is he lording it like a phantom king over the "democracy of the dead," which, as we said before, is Chesterton's definition of tradition? Entertaining all positions is a form of evasiveness; and in Eliot's solution to defining the use of literature we may detect a cold cosmopolitanism. What Chesterton said of Kipling comes to mind: "He lacks altogether the faculty of attaching himself to any cause of community finally and tragically; for all finality must be tragic."[6] Eliot, after a span of thirteen years as an American expatriate in London, made two serious commitments: to England and to its Church. But even as a British subject, he continued to see his place in society as a *metoikos* or sojourner. The parallel holds true for his place in literature. The poet Eliot remained aloof in mind from himself as a human person in the here and now. By wearing masks, he put art before nature. So I think it is with respect to the human nature of poetry that Eliot is most likely to go wrong. It is an ethereal spirit that says poetry is "not to be defined by its uses." It is, to concede Eliot's point, an earthen spirit that says poetry is "a criticism of life." It remains to be seen if there exists a viable alternative to these rival positions.

If an alternative is to be found, the tradition must supply a starting point. For Aristotle, the highest kinds or genres of poetry are tragic and epic. Of the two, he says tragedy is superior. It is more compact, more unified than narrative verse, and closer in terms of emotional effects to real life. But that is a relatively small matter. It will be sufficient if we extrapolate from Aristotle in several directions: our definition of poetry to include the highest prose, our conception of the highest genres to include the best novels, and our conception of the genres so as to be flexible and open to developments. Then, if we are true to the humanism of the *Poetics,* we must renew the ideal of fulfilling man's potential in the arts. Naturally, the best writers in the highest forms of literature will strive to realize this soulful capacity, in their work and in their characters, for the fullest expression of human nature would constitute the highest literary achievement.

I suggest that the best uses of literature share in this effort at completeness, which draws together the generations in an experience of mutual recognition. And with Eliot's warning about historical limitations in mind, we must add an important qualification: *the effort at*

6. Chesterton, *Collected Works,* 1:59.

completeness is always imperfect. All literature is a work in progress. It can hardly be overstated that no one has a "copyright" on human nature. Human nature is a universal idea, open to innumerable significant variations. The critic who enforces a strict paragon of human nature is policing infernal borders; if the image of Cerberus intrudes again, we are reminded that he has three heads.

What high art offers each generation is the chance for a new arrangement of powers, for truth, goodness, and beauty to be mutually revealed in a fresh light. And it is not a resolution of all contradictions, necessarily, but an original movement of thought and feeling that quickens vitality. Historically, our attempts at humanistic synthesis want to inspire a Renaissance. The possibility of future success hinges on our ability to recognize the conditions under which a movement toward synthesis can occur. In this respect, Arnold and Eliot concur: there must be "a current of ideas in the highest degree animating and nourishing to the creative power."[7] The best we can hope for is a rich dialogue of ideas, a synchronous opening of perception across a number of fields, that kindles the unifying powers of artistic genius.

Our present crisis of knowledge began in the nineteenth century, when logic broke from the Greeks, science expelled the ordinary educated person, and Lyell and Darwin shook the biblical faith in creation. Soon after, literature turned from mimesis; art turned from human form; and music turned from traditional tonality. Modernism made a last, courageous effort at a new synthesis, but the results, though often brilliant, were obscure. The modernists emulated the abstruseness of science, when the scientists themselves were struggling to bridge the moral gap between theory and practice.

The great physicist Edward Teller accused society of a bias against science, but he was ignorant of artistic developments in the culture around him. Apparently, he did not recognize the alliance of science and art that distinguishes the modernist period. Someone might have asked him, where did the word *quark* come from? He blamed "the intellectual leaders" for the poor reception of Einstein,[8] who in fact

7. Arnold, quoted in Eliot, *Sacred Wood,* xii.

8. Teller, quoted in Mary Palevsky, *Atomic Fragments: A Daughter's Questions,* 51.

had such tremendous cachet among artists and philosophers that Wyndham Lewis wrote a book in protest, *Time and Western Man*. Modernism in its dominant mode rejects the "soft romanticism" of Poe's "Sonnet—To Science" or Yeats's "Song of the Happy Shepherd," poems where science means being roused from pleasant dreams by cold analysis. From the early Eliot through Joyce and Woolf, high modernism pursued the new science like an infatuated lover. And to extend the metaphor, it desired what it could never grasp.

Theoretical scientists like Teller share with many aesthetes a sophisticated primitivism, which denies the moral authority of civilization (the Church was another target for Teller) in favor of the truth of pure form. This obsession with form cannot be dismissed as a private affair. "The chief forms of beauty," Aristotle says in the *Metaphysics*, "are order and symmetry and definiteness, which the mathematical sciences demonstrate in a special degree."[9] Whatever its limitations, Aristotle's feeling for the beauty of "the mathematical sciences" reminds us that science has its lovers and its priests. In the days of the pre-Socratics, poetry had a hunger for systematic cosmology and yearned to explore the nature of physical reality. If poetry is to regain that colossal appetite, it will have to find a way to digest modern physics. But the artistic obstacle is that the truth of pure form (for example, "string theory") is morally opaque; and in this respect, the abstract beauty of theoretical science commands our interest but not our love. Knowledge is power, said Bacon. But knowledge that cannot fit into a human story is dangerous. Facts without values are not quite human. In mythical language, they are monstrous or semidivine. The healthy imagination that sails within range of morality senses this dangerous power, lurking at the far edge of the world. Theoretical science cannot be colonized by human self-understanding, not even as an expression of our irrational desires, of our service to death or lust—the Freudian reading of Teller that Stanley Kubrick gives in *Dr. Strangelove*. It may respond to our compulsions, but so will the sun if we stare at it. To speak the language of humanism, truth must relate fact to value, information to wisdom, and science to humanity. New ideas in science can be mesmerizing, but is what follows, that is, the applied science, morally digestible? The challenge is to keep the fringe of the aesthetic

9. Aristotle, *Basic Works*, 893 (*Metaph.* 1078b).

and of science (modernism shows the two have something in common) in a humanizing perspective. The effort is generational. Like Odysseus or Gulliver, we should explore other scales of being and other orders of time. It is bracing to think that the Sirens have always been dangerous.

The *Poetics* establishes the relation between action and feeling as the fulcrum of humanistic literature. It is the primary support on which the meaning turns. It speaks to universal human nature, so that we can recognize in imaginative works an epitome of our moral lives. It is central to imitation or mimesis, which Aristotle views as the harmonious growth and completion of human nature. But all these terms—*character, epitome, mimesis*—are partial and incomplete, and Aristotle's view of human nature is itself incomplete.

The Christian belief in the reality of evil may be said to change the Aristotelian model from black and white into color. According to the *Poetics,* tragedy presents characters of the higher, comedy characters of the lower, type. Their respective motives and aims, virtues and vices, conform accordingly. In classical tragedy, the usurper or tyrant can achieve the imposing stature of Clytaemnestra or Cleon. The epic has its stock fools and clever liars, such as Thersites, Dolon, and Sinon. But Christianity gives even the villain new life. In Christian literature and in literature informed by Christianity, sin is surprisingly resourceful, from the Wife of Bath to Faust to Scrooge to Mr. Kurtz, whose name is an anagram for Christ. Sméagol or Gollum, whom Bilbo wisely spares, shows buried reserves of goodness—a latency all but unknown to the classical imagination. Though he does not in the end repent, Gollum plays his part in the comedy of Providence. Director Peter Jackson deserves credit for recognizing the comic possibilities of the character in his film adaptation.[10]

Christianity, it is said, is the religion of the second chance, and with Christianity arises that cosmic sense of comedy that Dante considered the essence of literature. This higher comedy flourishes in Chaucer, Cervantes, Shakespeare, and Dickens. It often exhibits a Pauline sense of faith's superabundant gift, the grace that redeems the sinner, exalts the lowly, and rescues the lost—as though Providence itself were a

10. It is interesting, by the way, how Jackson's Sauron resembles Emerson's transparent eyeball.

surprising comical genius with a flair for the absurd. Was Falstaff saved? No one can say, of course, but that possibility lingers in our minds. The dismal fate of Cambridge, Scroop, and Grey is structurally suggestive: it acts as a foil to our vision of Falstaff babbling "of green fields." Christianity gives to the foremost Christian writers an intensity and a reach that their classical counterparts lack, for there is now the drama of salvation haunting the proceedings. When imagination mediates between God and man, the union of biblical theology and Aristotelian ethics, that is, the marriage of Jerusalem and Athens happens (we say!) through this miraculous form of comic vision. It is found in *The Canterbury Tales* and *A Midsummer Night's Dream*. Fielding catches it in *Tom Jones,* as does Sterne in *Tristram Shandy.* It continues via Dickens into Chesterton. The closest American versions I know are in short stories by Fitzgerald and O'Connor. All these works and writers convey the Christian paradox of the comic destiny of man.

Characters spring to live by embodying ideals without being allegorically reduced to them. Dante's Beatrice, a high-minded Italian beauty *and* the embodiment of Divine Wisdom, is a prime example. But we may find ideals shining through particulars in the humblest circumstances. "The slum mother with her funerals is the degenerate daughter of Antigone," writes Chesterton. "The lady talking bad Italian was the decayed tenth cousin of Portia, the great and golden Italian lady, the Renascence amateur of life, who could be a barrister because she could be anything."[11] Antigone and Portia are not stock figures; they are realized with such particular intensity that they can speak, respectively, for the sad filial loyalty of the poor urbanite or the middling amateurism of "the elegant early Victorian female." And this particular intensity concentrates the moral imagination.

If Christianity is at home with truth and goodness, the Puritan revolt against Catholic idolatry suggests that beauty is a different matter. The Jews in the Old Testament have a passionate moral awareness of physical beauty, but their prohibition of graven images planted the seeds of Puritanism. In the New Testament, worldly beauty is only apparent. We hear of the deceptive beauty of sepulchers (Matt 23:27); and at a temple entrance called the Beautiful Gate, Peter and John miraculously heal a lame man (Acts 3:2 and 3:10). Their holy act puts

11. Chesterton, *What's Wrong,* 174.

the Beautiful Gate to shame. It is fair to say that suspicion of beauty runs high among Christians.

The western literary tradition, which Christianity has on the whole nourished and conserved, holds that beauty is realest (unlike Aphrodite) and best when connected to truth and goodness. Why doesn't Helen stop being beautiful when she leaves Sparta? Because Homer is attentive to her moral dignity; her beauty requires her nobler qualities. Priam and Hector exhibit their virtues through their kindness to her. And she is intensely self-critical. Dido is cut from the same cloth. Milton's Eve is a higher kind of Helen, for whom great beauty has a more developed spiritual pathos than aristocratic Greece could supply. Her type of moral ordeal or spiritual trial enters into such diverse characters as Francesca, Guenever, Gertrude, Hester Prynne, and Molly Bloom, all of whom are tempted and fall. By comparison, Shaw's Mrs. Warren is two-dimensional: a brilliant exercise in Fabian propaganda. Through Spenser's Duessa we learn the central Christian lesson about beauty: appearances can be deceiving. This inexhaustible lesson runs, along a wide and variegated range of responses to classical beauty, through Shakespeare, Austen, Dickens, Charlotte Brontë, Wilde, Chesterton, Eliot, Tolkien, Fitzgerald, Waugh, O'Connor, and Spark. Certainly, erotic beauty is philosophically potent: the parallel between the *Phaedrus* and the *Commedia* indicates this potency. But the physical incarnation of beauty in the world of time remains a human mystery that gives poets an honored name in the Church.

Humanism has in the past been associated with discredited forms of classicism, and it would be surprising if Christian humanism wholly escaped this problem.[12] Barzun observes the appeal of neoclassicism from the seventeenth through the twentieth century. Laws and conventions, he suggests, engender a system that "produces stability in the state and with it all the attributes of the static: fixed grandeur, dignity, authority, and high polish; while in an individual it produces morality and peace by showing him that values are rooted in the universe." Chesterton and Tolkien avoided this factitious charm, but Eliot succumbed in the late 1920s, describing his "general point of view . . . as classicist in literature, royalist in politics, and anglo-catholic in

12. In the language of earlier culture wars, the humanism of William James is romantic, the New Humanism of Irving Babbitt and P. E. More is classical.

religion." Shortly thereafter he abandoned the classicist pose, rightly concluding that he was romantic himself, and that his period was inevitably romantic.[13]

Both neoclassicism and romanticism have a tendency to impoverish time, resulting in the narrowing of perception and the stagnancy of ideas. I assume, in other words, a direct relation between our sense of time and our intellectual health. The vice of neoclassicism is to be backward looking: compulsively typical, fearful of dissonance, rule-bound. The vice of romanticism is to be baselessly progressive: radically individual, fearful of consensus, and hateful of convention. Either vice competes for cultural influence, defines the modern in its own light, and distorts the other in its own image.

In the radical middle, the Christian humanist wants to rectify these cultural time warps. Certainly the answer is not to subject literary taste to theological regulation. On the other hand, theological analogy is fair play in literary criticism, which is always, I maintain, *paratheological* and not *atheological.* I want to suggest that, practically speaking, the richest approach to this problem of time lies in the Trinitarian relation of the Father, the Son, and the Holy Spirit. I find my analogy in the Lesser Doxology, which is said in the rosary and in the liturgical hours: "Glory be to the Father, and to the Son, and to the Holy Spirit, as it was in the beginning, is now, and ever shall be." The parallel structure of this short prayer connects the *Father* with *the beginning,* the *Son* with *now,* and the *Holy Spirit* with *the future.* Through this interweaving of past, present, and future, where all three aspects of time focus our attention, a fuller understanding of history is possible, against which distortions emerge as heretical "time warps."

In Johnson's *Rasselas,* the sage Imlac holds that the poet must "rise to general and transcendent truths, which will always be the same." In his *Preface to Shakespeare,* Johnson explains why this is so: "Nothing can please many, and please long, but just representations of general nature."[14] Is Johnson static? Let us reject the charge that truth, just representations, and general nature are simply matters of convention: that is the way of nominalism and ideology. And yet we may feel that

13. Jacques Barzun, *Classic, Romantic, and Modern,* 36–37; T. S. Eliot, *For Lancelot Andrewes: Essays on Style and Order,* vii; Eliot, *Use of Poetry,* 121.

14. Johnson, *Selected Poetry and Prose,* 90, 301.

neoclassicism constructs its temple a little too ponderously. The beauty is predictable, the science is clockwork.

Johnson wanted literature to delight and instruct the reader, not to save or transform him. His image of man was somberly satirical: man as the plaything of fate. I quote from the *Idler,* one of the first major literary periodicals, with Johnson quoting Virgil:

> Those who have been able to conquer habit are like those that are fabled to have returned from the realms of Pluto:
>
> > Pauci, quos aequus amavit
> > Jupiter, atque ardens evexit ad aethera virtus.
> > [A few whom friendly Jupiter has loved
> > And ardent virtue has raised to the skies.]
> > (*Aeneid,* 6.129–30)
>
> They are sufficient to give hope but not security, to animate the contest but not to promise victory.[15]

This Johnsonian exegesis can be understood as a statement on the moral and spiritual limits of literature itself. Johnson leaves for Christianity the task of saving the many who cannot "conquer habit." It is literature that illuminates the need for Christianity, and not a weakness in Christianity that creates a need for literature. But though he is incisive, firm, and wise, we cannot say of Johnson, as Dryden said of Chaucer, that here is God's plenty. Man is more various and peculiar and hopeful than Johnson allows. Not only man, but creation itself. The shadow of a lack, which Chesterton noticed in Augustine, may be said to graze Johnson's noble visage. Chesterton noticed in Augustine "a mood which unconsciously committed the heresy of dividing the substance of the Trinity. It thought of God too exclusively as a Spirit who purifies or a Saviour who redeems; and too little as a Creator who creates." Johnson was more Christian than Deist, but he lived in a Deist century, and his work is deficient in Chesterton's Thomistic sense of "positive creation" that "is perpetually present."[16] He held back from Christian dynamism.

To "be a poet," writes Shelley in his *Defence of Poetry,* "is to apprehend the true and the beautiful, in a word the good which exists in

15. Samuel Johnson, *Selected Essays from the Rambler, Adventurer, and Idler,* 286.
16. Chesterton, *Collected Works,* 2:468.

the relation, substituting, first between existence and perception, and secondly between perception and expression." This text is difficult because the key terms *(the true, the good, the beautiful)* play a game of intellectual leapfrog. Truth and beauty are said to be intrinsic to uncorrupted existence. Goodness is what happens in the act of perceiving that existence (this unifying or synthesizing act is called "imagination"). Goodness, furthermore, is what happens through the act of expressing that perception. Shelley's *Defence* is therefore a theology of mediation: the poet's apprehension of true and beautiful relations (the living metaphors of an ultimate unity), and his expression of an unfallen world, mediate between that world and our own. It is a theology with something for everybody: the "tragedies of the Athenian poets are as mirrors in which the spectator beholds himself, under a thin disguise of circumstance, stript of all but that ideal perfection and energy which everyone feels to be the internal type of all that he loves, admires, and would become."[17] This is not Lear's "Off, off, you lendings!" It is not the recognition of "unaccommodated man." Quite the opposite. It is the recognition of unfallen man.

The great challenge posed by Shelley, an undeniable genius, lies in his heretical, quasi-gnostic imagination. Poets, he writes with youthful zeal, "draw into a certain propinquity with the beautiful and the true that partial apprehension of the agencies of the invisible world which is called religion." This access to "agencies" is important, for "the great instrument of moral good is the *imagination;* and poetry administers to the effect by acting upon the cause." But the poet himself is only a medium. He is not the final cause, which is a spiritual mystery: "for the mind in creation is as a fading coal which some invisible influence, like an inconstant wind, awakens to transitory brightness." This "invisible influence," wherever it comes from (the reader may be recalling Isaiah 6:6–7), stands behind Shelley's "attempt to idealize the modern forms of manners and opinion, and compel them into a subordination to the imaginative and creative faculty." Shelley's poets are not Johnsonian legislators handing down unchanging laws. They are at once "legislators or prophets" (the "or" is a typical Shelleyan unifying of alternatives). The poet "not only beholds intensely the present as it is, and discovers those laws according to which present things *ought* to be ordered, but he beholds the future in the present, and his

17. Percy Bysshe Shelley, *Shelley's Poetry and Prose,* 482, 490.

thoughts are the germs of the flower and the fruit of latest time." Poets, in the long view, "are the institutors of the laws, and the founders of civil society and the inventors of the arts of life." Finally, the Deweyan pragmatist will commend Shelley's judgment that poetry "comprehends all science," for Shelley inspires and dignifies Dewey's contention that all knowledge is social technology, or "power" in the Baconian sense that Shelley and Dewey echo.[18]

As a modern version of romance, romanticism is a means for the arts to return—through the wilderness of modernity—to their home in the life of man. In this sense Christian humanism is more romantic than it is medieval, neoclassical, or modernist: Chesterton, Eliot, and Tolkien bequeath a romantic legacy to the Church. And in this respect, Wordsworth, who occupies the hard-to-hold ground between the neoclassicism of Johnson and the ultraromanticism of Shelley, beckons with paternal authority. Wordsworth's great *Ode* is a synthesis of experience and vision, an interweaving of past, present, and future, and a defense of faith and reason: "We will grieve not, rather find / Strength in what remains behind . . . / In the soothing thoughts that spring / Out of human suffering / In the faith that looks through death, / In years that bring the philosophic mind."[19] Wordsworth's "faith" is not closed to Christianity, it is intentionally open to Christianity, and that is probably why so much critical effort has been expended on making him non-Christian; it is probably why the 1850 *Prelude*, a masterpiece by any measure whatsoever, has been neglected by anti-Christian critics in favor of the 1805 manuscript.[20]

The later Eliot defers to Wordsworth's "version of Imitation," where the poet has "an ability of conjuring up in himself passions, which are indeed far from being the same as those produced by real events, yet . . . do more nearly resemble the passions produced by real events, than anything which, from the motions of their own minds merely, other men are accustomed to feel in themselves." Shelley, by comparison, describes the poet's work as in essence spiritualized, which is to say, he is ideally disembodied. In this respect and others, he haunts Eliot's imagination. He breaks from the "orthodox" position that Eliot, in a crucial passage,

18. Ibid., 482, 488 (italics mine), 503–4, 507, 482, 482–83 (italics mine), 482, 503.
19. William Wordsworth, *Poetical Works,* 462.
20. See William A. Ulmer, *The Christian Wordsworth, 1798–1805.*

attributes to Wordsworth: "in the matter of mimesis he is more deeply Aristotelian than some who have aimed at following Aristotle more closely." We may sense that the "some" under review includes Eliot's younger self. For Shelley, the "story of particular facts is as a mirror which obscures and distorts that which should be beautiful: Poetry is a mirror which makes beautiful that which is distorted." This resembles Wordsworth's observation, based on Aristotle (and admired by Eliot), that poetry's "object is truth, not individual and local, but general, and operative." But to discern the humanization or dehumanization of truth, goodness, and beauty, we must study what happens in the mimetic realm of the body. Upon inspection, we find that Wordsworth treats the body very differently from how Shelley treats it. Wordsworth is a mimetic author for whom truth, goodness, and beauty are realized in the flesh. One thinks of "Tintern Abbey," *Michael,* most of *The Prelude,* and most of *The Excursion,* including its superb first book, the story of Margaret. The exceptions are important. They stem from Wordsworth's devotion to nature at a time in England when the flame of faith burned low. They stem also from spiritual gifts that Arnold failed to appreciate, and that Eliot, possessed of similar gifts, related in his own case to the mystery of salvation. Shelley is heretical on the whole. He is neither mimetic in his art, nor incarnational in his poetic theology. His chiastic mirror image ("distorts . . . beautiful . . . beautiful . . . distorted") is no accident, for the mirror is central to Shelley's vision: the "tragedies of the Athenian poets are as mirrors in which the spectator beholds himself." Poets are "the mirrors of the gigantic shadows which futurity casts upon the present." These mirrors are an idealistic medium, the nexus of timeless spirit and time-bound things. For Shelley, a heretical spirit absorbs the fallen creation, even as it (the spirit) casts its bodiless images back at us: "Reason is to Imagination, as the instrument to the agent, as the body to the spirit, as the shadow to the substance."[21] Facts, habits, and traditions are transformed beyond recognition into a future that sheds them like a chrysalis. There is no love between past, present, and future, no reciprocity, only an imperial future where truth is final, goodness beyond reason, and beauty fleshless.

21. Wordsworth, quoted in Eliot, *Use of Poetry,* 66; Eliot, *Use of Poetry,* 65; Shelley, *Shelley's Poetry and Prose,* 485; Wordsworth, quoted in Eliot, *Use of Poetry,* 66; Shelley, *Shelley's Poetry and Prose,* 508, 480.

I will have more to say about romanticism in the final chapter, but here I want to linger over the well-established connection between romanticism and democracy. We have, as points of reference, the authority of Wordsworth and Eliot on this subject, which occupies the Preface to *Lyrical Ballads* and Eliot's discussion of Wordsworth in *The Use of Poetry and the Use of Criticism*. I want to suggest that, through romanticism, western art and democracy have entered into a spiritual compact and cultural marriage—till death do them part. I speak of a spiritual solidarity, which can support a workable conception of human rights. For us all, sharing a world that is increasingly interdependent, the romantic legacy in the West culminates in an epochal choice: either to rectify our perspectives on past, present, and future, and so to keep the humanistic vision alive, or to abandon this trinity for arrangements that seem safer or more progressive.

At the heart of this project is a fine recognition of the true needs of the individual. If you want to know what the future may look like, totalitarian democracy is enjoying a test run wherever "the debauching of the arts by political criteria" passes for excellence.[22] The art of literature, on the other hand, has always succeeded by heralding the individual in writing, according to criteria such as style, genius, and the classic. The life and history of a particular writer also color our judgment of his or her accomplishment. This appreciation of the individual, the harmony and tension traced by Eliot in "Tradition and the Individual Talent," has a foundation that the early Eliot sometimes obscured. The aesthetic humanism of *The Sacred Wood* is akin, in period and outlook, to the relativist type of modernism that, shedding the burden of traditional learning, gave rise to postmodernism(-isms) (whatever). Concealed in this antihumanist environment is the created order, the cosmos where reason and nature can serve as guides to the good life. Almost by definition, this life, the historic life of culture where goodness and truth and beauty are richly interwoven in their superabundant variety, recognizes the individual achievement in art; for in art the depth and vision of the individual soul are revealed. In other words, the substance of art has something to do with the substance of each woman and man, with a mysterious essence that integrates form and matter. And so it is to the meaning of form that we now turn.

22. Eliot, *Idea of a Christian Society*, 34.

9

THE CANON AND LITERARY FORM

The formation of a canon serves to safeguard a tradition." So writes the distinguished philologist Ernst Robert Curtius in his classic study *European Literature and the Latin Middle Ages.* Curtius observes three major areas of canon formation: "the literary tradition of the school, the juristic tradition of the state, and the religious tradition of the Church." Canon formation takes place under numerous subheadings within each of these three major areas. The medieval Church, for example, reached agreement on the Ordinary of the Mass, the catalog of saints, church writers, and canon law. Invariably there was an element of happenstance in the selection process. "At the Council of Trent," Curtius informs us, "the Old Testament canon was established as dogma, but three apocryphal books of the Vulgate were added because they were cited in the writings of the Fathers." No *a priori* laws exist to guide the act of canon formation (in fact a few early Christians bypassed any written Gospel at all in favor of oral testimony). In the area of literary tradition, canon formation "must always proceed to a selection of classics."[1] But the ends to which literary study is directed, and therefore the meaning of a given classic, continue to change. The permanent elements emerge in dialogue with the past, and safeguarding the tradition becomes the work of time.

In this chapter I examine the role of literary form in canon formation. The close connection between the canon and literary form was well observed by Arnold in his landmark essay of 1879, "The Study of Poetry." George Saintsbury followed suit with his admirable (and

1. Ernst Robert Curtius, *European Literature and the Latin Middle Ages,* 256, 259.

not so short) *Short History of English Literature,* published in 1898. But in the period of vers libre, the connection between canonicity and form is pushed aside, when it is not ignored and forgotten.

Eliot is guilty of the push. In a 1917 essay, "Reflections on 'Vers Libre,'" he writes:

> the most interesting verse which has yet been written in our language has been done either by taking a very simple form, like the iambic pentameter, and constantly withdrawing from it, or taking no form at all, and constantly approximating to a very simple one. It is this contrast between fixity and flux, this unperceived evasion of monotony, which is the very life of verse.[2]

Let us reflect: *the most interesting verse.* After that little thunderbolt, the idea that iambic pentameter is "very simple" barely skims the reader's attention. Nineteen seventeen was the year of *Prufrock and Other Observations,* a demanding year for the young American in England. In order to establish his use of the new form, Eliot needed to attack the authority of the iambic pentameter line. He needed to reconfigure the canon while insisting, against the grain of Georgian sensibility, on his relation to it.

Eliot is unique in this: his extreme formal iconoclasm is correlative—inversely correlative—to his being extremely haunted by the past: "the ghost of some simple metre should lurk behind the arras in even the 'freest' verse; to advance menacingly when we doze, and withdraw as we rouse."[3] It will be evident that "simple" in the hands of Eliot is a dangerous word. Only the dead have ghosts. As for "simple," traditional meter is simple in the way that domes and columns are simple, which is to say, it makes a profoundly graceful claim on our attention. I have never seen an architect write off the classical orders as simple.[4] Good formal verse, far from being simple to write, is a challenge to whoever tries a hand at it. It is hard to write even marginally well, it blocks the impulse of direct self-expression, and it cruelly exposes inadequacies of training and sensibility. When he wanted to, Eliot wrote brilliant formal verse, which, perversely, gave his critics

---

2. Eliot, *To Criticize the Critic,* 185.
3. Ibid., 187.
4. See, for example, Arthur Stratton, *The Orders of Architecture.*

the excuse to dismiss him "as a Wit or a satirist."[5] The dismissal was unwarranted, but Eliot was outmatched by Hardy and Yeats, and later by Auden, in the field of formal verse. His original genius lay elsewhere.

Eliot defends his poetic by carefully building on the associations of *libre:* "freedom is only truly freedom when it appears against the background of an artificial limitation."[6] I hesitate again, because the limitations of poetry are not always "artificial." I agree with Eliot that limitation is necessary. But Aristotle saw a natural appropriateness, emerging from a history of trial and error, in how certain meters fit certain genres. This natural meetness of form and matter is not what Eliot had in mind when he wrote "Reflections on 'Vers Libre.'" More philosophically, his use of the word *artificial* evokes the idealist legacy of Kant, which operates in the modernist exclusion of nature. Eliot's modernist tendencies carry him, as usual, away from Aristotle.

I am inclined to Aristotle's view. The notion of artificial limits suggests that such limits are entirely conventional, when artistic limits often are not. It must be pleasing to invent a form of light verse:

> Sir Humphrey Davy
> Detested gravy.
> He incurred the odium
> Of discovering sodium.[7]

Chesterton took the lesson from his fellow schoolboy, Edmund Clerihew Bentley, and a host of clerihews sprang into being. But it is a different order of experience when a serious verse form takes root in the soil of a maturing culture, which craves the fruit of poetic expression. It is inconceivable that clerihew-style doggerel could sustain a tragedy. By virtue of nature itself, the iambic pentameter is much better suited for tragedy and epic in English. It is not the only possible meter (as *Murder in the Cathedral* demonstrates); and the classical genres are serviceable in only a loose and suggestive way. Metrical form is an approximate measure for speech that is always changing. It is artis-

5. Eliot, *Letters,* 1:363.
6. Eliot, *To Criticize the Critic,* 187.
7. Edmund Clerihew Bentley, quoted in Chesterton, *Collected Works,* 16:64.

tic, not purely mathematical, in design, intended to embody and not to dictate expression. That other metrical possibilities exist, beyond the adaptations of classical scansion that reflect traditional humanistic thinking on the subject, I happily accept as true. Their existence can only complement, and by no means contradict, the gist of my argument, since I am eager to cultivate all species of poetry. The main idea is that reason and nature combine in suggesting the form and therefore the formal limits that characterize these species.

For confirmation from a mind worth knowing, it will be helpful to delve into the unduly neglected work of Saintsbury, whose practical approach to "the genius of English poetry" applies to the best poetry of all times and all languages.[8] Saintsbury observes the natural development of English poetry after Chaucer. I quote him at length, because the point in question requires his narrative to be appreciated:

> certainly it would appear that Chaucer's English is in a state of premature and forced perfection to which his successors could not attain, and which, before any fit heir appeared, became archaic. It would appear likewise that the completion of the constitution of English proper, the final severance from the Continent, and the changes of which the disappearance of the final *e* is the most remarkable, had brought about, or had at least been followed by, some not clearly intelligible change in the whole tonality and vocalisation of the tongue. The new pronounced English was not adjustable to Chaucerian prosody, and it did not find what it wanted in alliterative verse. The results were that extraordinary stumbling and plunging, that driving of the chariot as if with locked wheels, . . . in Lydgate, in Occleve, and even in Hawes, . . . from which Skelton only escaped (when he did escape) by a series of clumsy gambades in doggerel. Yet this doggerel did good by teaching the language at least to move with some flexibility, if with little elegance. . . . [T]hese stumbles were inevitable in picking the way up the steep and stony path from the abysses to which English poetry had descended, and the very stumbles themselves are gain, inasmuch as they warn the stumbler to pick his way more carefully next time. Wyatt has the plain, straight, and strait ways of the sonnet and other forms to guide him.[9]

8. George Saintsbury, *A History of English Literature: Elizabethan Literature,* 9.
9. George Saintsbury, *A Short History of English Literature,* 246–47.

The process that Saintsbury describes is a study in reason and nature. It reflects much the same grappling with trial and error that Aristotle perceived among the post-Homeric poets. Before the time of *Tottel's Miscellany* (1557), early modern English was falling into place and slowly growing more tunable and flexible. A few minor poets left their mark. (Skelton is elsewhere said to represent "the English tendency to prosaic doggerel.")[10] At the dawn of the English Renaissance, the fine problems of prosody and rhyme awaited the geniuses who would solve them.

We find the English canon secured by two poets with the power to rival Homer and Virgil. In Shakespeare and Milton, the enormous potential of the iambic pentameter is made evident and magnificently realized. The iambic tetrameter, which tends toward a different order of feeling and content (it is less appropriate for the highest actions), finds its representatives among less ambitious poets. This process of classification points to a rudimentary first principle of canon formation. The best literature, I suggest, has a natural basis in creative intelligence that grasps what form can do. And it should be borne in mind that form is inseparable from reason, and that all creativity has a mathematical and logical side to it. History has a say, moreover, and there are times when the best writers must let the richest fields lie fallow, because either the language and its rhythms are changing, or (as Eliot suggests of Virgil) someone has harvested a moment of ripeness, or some cultural shock has radically disturbed our relations to the past. Modernism in poetry is probably the natural result of all three causes; someday it may take definitive shape as an offshoot from the main line.

From a broad perspective, Eliot's innovations show canonicity and form to be closely related. The tragic closure of "The Love Song of J. Alfred Prufrock" intensifies the aura of Shakespearean tragedy that elevates the poem's denouement. Not only Prince Hamlet, but the pentameter of Hamlet's dying words, confer a high pathos on Prufrock's demise: "Till human voices wake us and we drown." The reader steps in to play the part of Horatio: "Now cracks a noble heart. Good night, sweet prince, / And flights of angels sing thee to thy rest!"[11] This resource of cultural literacy, of readerly friendship in the knowledge of poetic form, is a sign that poetry is flourishing. To clarify the point,

10. Saintsbury, *History of English Literature*, 5.
11. William Shakespeare, *The Riverside Shakespeare*, 1185.

I offer another example of what is at stake, from one of Eliot's minor gems, "Lines for Cuscuscaraway and Mirza Murad Ali Beg":

> How unpleasant to meet Mr. Eliot!
> With his features of clerical cut,
> And his brow so grim
> And his mouth so prim . . .[12]

Eliot is denying us the satisfaction of a dactylic adjective (for instance, "wopsical") before the unadorned "features" of line two. We want and expect four beats in line two, an expectation raised by the choric opening line, which, strictly speaking, has an anaepestic rhythm of three beats, but which allures us with its illusory, super-anaepestic opulence:

> /   /   /   /   /   /
> How unpleasant to meet Mr. Eliot!

After this whetting of the tongue, the poet defeats our rhythmic desire with his austere execution. The lines that follow are likewise "prim," "[r]estricted," and "unpleasant" as any Puritan could want. Talk about dry wit.

Can Eliot, like Wordsworth, be said to have created the taste by which he is enjoyed? It is a delicate question whether he should be credited with a refinement or with a revolution of taste. To be sure, he took part in the movement that Ezra Pound spearheaded. He made it new, but not as new as William Carlos Williams, remembering 1922, would have liked:

> Out of the blue *The Dial* brought out *The Waste Land* and all our hilarity ended. It wiped out our world as if an atom bomb had been dropped on it and our brave sallies into the unknown were turned to dust.
> . . . Critically Eliot returned us to the classroom just at the moment when I felt that we were on the point of an escape to matters much closer to the essence of a new art form itself.[13]

---

12. Eliot, *Collected Poems,* 137.
13. William Carlos Williams, *Autobiography,* 174.

All of Williams is a falling off from one superbly accomplished experiment: the first poem from the sequence entitled *Spring and All*. Much
of Williams is pleasurable reading, but he never again succeeded in
achieving a "new art form" with the organic intensity of that finest
poem. Pound (who is the real butt of Williams's *Autobiography*) meets
the impossible standards of his friend more than anyone else. But Eliot
was not quite playing Pound's or Williams's game. His voice is more
elegiac than theirs, and this elegiac quality affects our understanding
of his form. He is not a traditional poet, he is a poet of the tradition.

Despite some important periods of formalist revival, vers libre has
more or less dominated the poetry magazines for about a century.
Chesterton was lampooning free verse as early as *The Flying Inn*. But
after so many years, we ought to distinguish between the thrill of formal liberation and the realization of formal potential. Then we can see
that the growth in *formal realization,* which happens in the English
Renaissance, from the beginnings of the English sonnet in Wyatt and
Surrey to the heights of Shakespeare and Milton, has no parallel in free
verse. The publicity machine is of course in high gear. More and more
books appear, while the art of poetry continues its recession from public consciousness. The "real estimate," Arnold stubbornly points out,
"is liable to be superseded . . . by two other kinds of estimate, the historic estimate and the personal estimate, both of which are falla-
cious."[14] Certainly vers libre or (synonymously) free verse or open form
possesses great historical interest. Its ablest defenders pay attention to
history. But the real estimate is strictly out of bounds. Go there, and
a professional writers' guild will judge that you are insensitive (or
worse) to meaningful new art. So artistic justice is denied to Milton
(Shakespeare is deified and ignored), since that is what the real estimate is, an ideal of artistic justice, delayed but not destroyed. It will
not matter that Milton was a genius whose work is good for your brain.
The establishment is liberated from the regime of Milton, just as it is
liberated from reason, nature, and the God of the Christians. And it
must be admitted that the establishment has a point. Nature, reason,
and the God of the Christians do in fact keep close company.

When free verse escapes the cut and stamp of mass production, a
humanistic impulse prevails. In a few exceptional cases, free verse has

14. Arnold, *Complete Prose Works,* 9:163.

fostered the rare element of individuality in art. These exceptional cases, even the most deliberately American, harken back to the Italian Renaissance, the high summer of artistic canonization, and to its gorgeous English autumn. Even in the wintry days of modernism and its aftermath, the love of form drives the superior artist.

But the suspicion lingers that free verse is often parasitical, dependent on a positive principle of form that it cannot define or supply. It is striking, for instance, that free verse achieves many distinctive effects through pruning. Eliot's manuscripts give evidence of this: the mature poem is often smaller, sometimes much smaller, than in adolescence. The risk, overcome by Eliot through his almost unerring powers of lyrical suggestion, is that a minimalist and fastidious art will narrow the spectrum of thought and feeling. After carting off the dead wood of poetic convention, the free verse writer may find that he has all along been hacking at the root.

A further necessary distinction is between open form, which affords the possibility of artistic mastery, and antiformalism, which does not. Antiformalism is an aspect of aesthetic antihumanism. A good example is John Ashbery's "This Room," which treats the universal theme of hospitality. In a formal pun, the poet *almost* begins his verses with iambic pentameter, but the line lands heavily, like a bottom step being missed:

> The room I entered was a dream of this room.
> Surely all those feet on the sofa were mine.
> The oval portrait
> of a dog was me at an early age.
> Something shimmers, something is hushed up.
>
> We had macaroni for lunch every day
> except Sunday, when a small quail was induced
> to be served to us. Why do I tell you these things?
> You are not even here.[15]

Ashbery is a literary gnostic: he makes no claim to theological knowledge, but excludes the uninitiated with an impenetrable code. The poem is an antiformalist cryptogram: (1) room=stanza; (2) feet on sofa=*informal* meter; (3) portrait of young dog=the post-Joycean artist

15. John Ashbery, *Your Name Here*, 3.

(by way of Dylan Thomas); (4) shimmering and hushing=experience
of reading or writing (not speaking or reciting) poetry; (5) maca-
roni=macaronics and dandyism; (6) Sunday=absurd ritual of art; (7)
quail=wandering in the desert (Exodus 16:13); (8) I=You, in a book
called *Your Name Here,* in which the death of the author happens with
every poem, if not every line. Hospitality hinges on a correct interpretation of the code, which ushers in the initiated and shuts out everybody else. The problem facing the reader is that there are no discernable
social relations: the poem in its emotional obscurity walls out the complex and often dangerous reality of host and guest. It is nonmimetic,
a surreal and remarkably specialized bag of tricks. Whether its twinge
of affect is compassionate, despairing, whimsical, or cynical, who can
say? The corrosive effect of Ashbery's poetry is that it makes the family of man, whose moral life is the subject of mimetic art, a cliché or
stock figure of ridicule, much as Hazlitt imagined the urban sophis-
ticate laughing at the country bumpkin.

With gnosis shouldering out high art, the journey from ultraso-
phistication to rank incompetence has been abrupt. Our tastemakers
have privileged open form at the same time that they have lost their
sense of traditional form—what I have called "readerly friendship." No
doubt, formal proficiency can disguise a lack of heart. But our estrangement from traditional form means an estrangement from nature, and
that means a decline in sociability:

> Chip the glasses and crack the plates!
> Blunt the knives and bend the forks!
> That's what Bilbo Baggins hates—
> Smash the bottles and burn the corks![16]

I have remembered this all my life. Its boisterous ease is exactly appropriate to the emotion, which is not so simple, after all: the guests are
literally playing on the fears of the host, marking the important social
distinction between play and violence. The end rhymes seem to catch
the very items that are in peril. But the surprising guests, being civilized, clean everything up and put it neatly away.

Words are not tokens floating in the Void. Rather, words are
grounded in the history of man, sacred and secular. Ordinary words

16. J. R. R. Tolkien, *The Hobbit,* 19.

have a secret life, reaching out to each other through subtle, often unconscious, channels and associations. The good writer is, among other things, the chronicler of this life. "Soap" is a cleaner, but it can suggest soap operas and soap boxes, which are ways of getting the dirt or dishing it out. The social relations of man are inseparable from the reality of words. But if the natural or literal significance of words is lost through sophistication or propaganda, their human potential is severely reduced. Our mythical horse must have his wings clipped. "Mr. Shaw and Mr. Wells," Eliot observes, "are . . . much occupied with religion and *Ersatz-Religion.* But they are concerned with the spirit, not the letter. And the spirit killeth, but the letter giveth life."[17] The sentiment is not legalistic. In his playful (and orthodox) inversion of Saint Paul (see 2 Corinthians 3:6), Eliot makes the Chestertonian point that false prophets threaten the arts with destruction. The gemlike flame of decadence is never more consuming than when anti-Christian writers squander meaning and obviate sense. Without the capacity for literalness, conserved by Christianity through the offices of reason and nature, literature shades into ideology, language games, and formlessness. The best modernist poetry, including *The Waste Land,* makes a virtue of conditions that are challenging to say the least. What we find over decades of free verse, however, is this: an art that has no formal principle tends to elide reason, nature, and history.

A word or two about fiction, at least to suggest how the connection between the canon and literary form might apply in this area, is in order. Being highly social in nature, fiction gradually loses form and expressiveness as writers grow estranged from society. Here too we must be careful to separate the thrill of the new, especially in the hands of brilliant innovators, from the realization of a form's expressive potential. Joyce and Chekhov developed a new form, a masterful sketch of character that winnows traditional social relations like chaff from the grain of art. A fully realized form, like a life, has a beginning, a middle, and an end. But beginnings do not know their ends in works like Joyce's "Eveline" and Chekhov's "The Lady with the Dog." In Chekhov's tale, which Virginia Woolf praised for its delicate portrayal of the soul, the protagonist is transformed by his adulterous love for a young provincial: "he judged of others by himself, not believing in what he saw, and

17. Eliot, *For Lancelot Andrewes,* 94n.

always believing that every man had his real, most interesting life under the cover of secrecy and under the cover of night."[18] Chekhov was calling into question the hypocritical need for "two lives," where the authoritarian public realm is all hollow convention, totally inauthentic, and private life is the refuge of truth. His lovers escape the swirl and wreckage of their past and embrace an unknown future. Joyce's Eveline lacks the daring to join her lover at the end; a hopeless Catholic, she sacrifices too much for her selfish father. In its raw intimacy, the form appears to be liberating. It strikes us as deeply humane, it wins us at a blow, but something somewhere has gone cold. The promise of human nature has been traded for an incommensurable soulful longing, a revelatory hidden passion that is spiritually aloof from the moment and place of its own consequences.

Czarist authoritarianism stands for the world, Catholic authoritarianism stands for the world, and the eagerness with which free societies in the West adopted the new models of self-liberation is a story of the enchantment of art. But art cannot survive by cannibalizing human nature. The psychological flame of liberation, sparked by Nietzsche and Freud, goes out if we disengage all social order and cosmic authority. Because this kind of change occurs over generations, it may elude our immediate perception. Chesterton, who picked up on these things, observed people becoming "inhuman out of sheer humanitarianism." It is arguable, we find, that the success of style over morality has reinforced (and been reinforced by) the success of humanitarianism over common sense. Studying this phenomenon, James Schall offers an unusual perspective on recent cultural history. The key idea is the vow as the test of character. The modern mind, with its refined aesthetic-humanitarian complex, has rejected this test. Writes Schall: "our culture has come to accept the breaking of vows and to call it romance, when their keeping was the only romance worth having." Described as being "passive, like a helpless animal," Joyce's Evelyn is a fool (not a saint) for honoring "her promise to her mother, her promise to keep the home together as long as she could."[19] By the same token, Chekhov's lovers are romantic heroes for breaking their

18. Anton Chekhov, *The Tales of Chekhov*, 3:25.

19. James V. Schall, *Schall on Chesterton: Timely Essays on Timeless Paradoxes*, 194; James Joyce, *Dubliners*, 40–41.

wedding vows. The cultural effects of such moral-aesthetic experiments do not vindicate the experimenters. Romance takes to its deathbed when the artists replace the priests, and the mystical bond between the sexes falls entirely under aesthetic supervision. Aestheticism chips away at love; its fragments are enshrined until their aura wanes. In a few generations, modern (or postmodern) art prohibits traditional romance as a cliché: society comes to uphold the authoritarianism that it originally rebelled against.

The dissolution of form and sense is likewise felt in the novel. F. Scott Fitzgerald was a sublime genius of style. He departed from the give-and-take of Catholic family life in order to pursue the lyric intensities of his prose, whose primary occasion was sundering the mind from the body of its past relations. He had rare gifts, a superb sense of plot and timing, comic genius at the end, and his wreck of a life was a romantic tragedy. But the drama of failure lost its form, and the pathos faded, as the Christian background (the liturgical calendar, family-centered morality, the Bible) suffered neglect. Possibly it was too little, too late when Woolf realized the truth of the matter in her surprising last novel, *Between the Acts*. While rethinking her antipathy for traditional plots, she embraced (or at least shook hands with) the Anglican tradition, in the hope that it could answer the threats posed by modernity, including Nazism. The novel ends in almost ceremonial deference to traditional marriage, without sacrificing Woolf's defiant moral intelligence. The postwar novelist is generally beyond good and evil, a voyeuristic exile without hope or nostalgia, prone to dark humor and stark reportage. The traditional plot is now largely in the hands of the multicultural school, whose approach to literature is chiefly propagandistic. Modeling the politically correct virtues, it bolsters the diversity regime that funds it, especially in state-funded primary and secondary education.[20]

Carried to perfection, the flawless surface of a pure style is a medium without a message. Its desirability, as the polestar of much postmodern writing, is a legacy of aestheticism, which was always in rebellion against reality. Stylistic genius can overcome the divorce between form and sense for a time, until human nature loses interest. Critics write

20. See Carol Iannone, "Reading Literature: Decline and Fall"; and Phillips, *Londonistan*.

with their heads but readers read with their hearts. And that is why Tolkien attracts such extremes of love and hate. I suspect it will be the abject coarseness of what is now following our ultrasophisticated postmodernism, descending on readers' heads like Yahoo excrement, that will inspire a full critical reevaluation of Tolkien, a writer who integrated form and sense, style and substance, while authoring a permanent new genre.

The religious significance of artistic form is a subject that can be difficult to teach. Either students come prepared to develop a religious sense of form, because they have the necessary background, or they will hardly be moved to consider the spiritual significance of form at all. Pugin's ideas were not received in a vacuum. His principles of architecture were consistent with his militant Catholicism. His love of his materials, his rich functionalism, his morality, his individuality: all reflect his tradition. First, Ruskin and Morris, then, Chesterton and Tolkien, grasped the religious element in Gothic, and learned from it. Until recently, established poets were deeply sensitive to religion. It is obvious that our forward-thinking universities have made orthodoxy taboo. And now our elite students are generally ignorant of Christianity. The entire tradition, Beckett included, is therefore largely incomprehensible to them.

That we did not make breath or silence, that we did not make sound or rhyme, that we did not make our freedom: these facts are the sacred ground of the canon and literary form. There is a very lively sense in which form brings home the farthest limits of our striving: the horizons of death and birth. Life is full of limits: form is good at interpreting and enacting them. Life is full of surprises: form is good at capturing them. Form and pattern invite contemplation, as well as a much fuller sense of time's interrelations than can be developed in a world where time is money.

Over the past decades, theorists have remorselessly deconstructed the kind of argument from reason and nature on which I have built my case for literary form.[21] I can fairly be accused of trying to revive a critical sensibility that has been buried under a heap of meaningless books, even as the canon itself has faded into oblivion or been diver-

---

21. A classic of the genre is Jacques Derrida, "The Supplement of Copula: Philosophy *before* Linguistics."

sified out of existence. Even so, to glimpse the old foundations, it is helpful to observe that Coleridge on form thoroughly complements the narrative of literary history laid out after him by Saintsbury:

> The form is mechanic when on any given material we impress a predetermined form, not necessarily arising out of the properties of the material, as when to a mass of wet clay we give whatever shape we wish it to retain when hardened. The organic form, on the other hand, is innate; it shapes as it develops itself from within, and the fullness of its development is one and the same with the perfection of its outward form.[22]

The point has been argued by Bate, but it bears repeating in this context, that Coleridge writes in the tradition of Aristotle.[23] So does Saintsbury. Both address the relation of matter to form, and both hold up the union of matter and form as their ideal. These issues are open to considerable complication, since the distinction between organic and mechanical, like everything else in literary criticism, is not final. For instance, it can be said that the comical potential of mechanical form is partly realized in the clerihew. More, literature can be deliberately mechanical, sometimes in defiance of such dualisms as mechanical-organic, and sometimes in general defiance of humanizing literature. But the terms are useful anyway: they are practical and wise.

The old foundations are not in ruins. Practical wisdom is not a nostalgia trip. Nor is theory, in the true sense of the word, blind to the best ends of life. All are joined in a larger picture, each enhancing the other, and all inspiring the romance of history. And that is the story of our last chapter.

22. Samuel Taylor Coleridge, *Shakespearean Criticism,* 1:198.
23. See Walter Jackson Bate, *Coleridge,* 149–53.

10

THE ROMANCE OF HISTORY

Chesterton's wisdom is a source of perpetual delight. While the disillusioned aesthete grew bored with others, Chesterton reached the conclusion of "a joke" against himself. "I am the man," he said, "who with the utmost daring discovered what had been discovered before."[1] This comical victory makes light of personal struggle, as it recovers the lost self almost accidentally. But Chesterton's heroic courage led him to realize his destiny in the harrowing consciousness of history.

Despite his ingrained aestheticism, Eliot came to uphold a Chestertonian view of romance. In *Four Quartets,* he likewise "discovered what had been discovered before":

> We shall not cease from exploration
> And the end of all our exploring
> Will be to arrive where we started
> And know the place for the first time.[2]

As always in *Four Quartets,* the word *end* is ambiguous. The soul longs for an ending that makes sense. But the promise of a full and unified meaning is continually deferred in Eliot's poetry. Even at the very end it is cast into the future. One of the most memorable phrases in the *Quartets* suggests why this is so: "humility is endless." It is a thought that strips the world away, until the soul moves precariously over the Void. Eliot uses his artistic mastery to pursue a spiritual askesis, where

---

1. Chesterton, *Collected Works,* 1:214.
2. Eliot, *Collected Poems,* 208.

turning from the self is paradoxically the means to self-realization. He cannot move directly toward God, but God is the end of his meditation.

Eliot's poetic surrender to the will of God resembles Gandalf's faith in the Hobbits' all-but-impossible errand. In both cases, the expression of humility is an expression of faith in the Christian myth of history. Both Eliot and Tolkien attend to a difficult balance, which requires constant fine adjustment between heroic striving and heroic surrender. Eliot's mediation between the still point and historical events reflects this adjustment, as does the narrative complexity of *The Lord of the Rings*. Both writers imply that humility means faith in Providence; they mystically experience the soul's freedom in the providential narrative that is God's word.

Eliot was between the wars when he described a descent into the abyss: "Desiccation of the world of sense, / Evacuation of the world of fancy, / Inoperancy of the world of spirit." It is no accident that these verses from the third section of "Burnt Norton" evoke Frodo's ordeal on the plains of Mordor, in sight of Mount Doom: "No taste of food, no feel of water, no sound of wind, no memory of tree or grass or flower, no image of moon or star are left me."[3] For all intents and purposes, Eliot and Tolkien represent the same historical crisis and spiritual need. Sam Gamgee returns to life in the Shire much as Eliot returns to "the children in the apple-tree." It is a romantic pattern of homecoming, the intense last test or crucible of romanticism, which in its final affirmative phase returns modernity to its Christian roots. This is true in the individual careers of Wordsworth, Coleridge, and Eliot; the negative phase that we see, for instance, in Shelley's *Triumph of Life* is something that Eliot accepts and works through.

Against the tradition that I am defending, the modernist school has leveled the charge that it is childish. Edmund Wilson called *The Lord of the Rings* "juvenile trash." Edwin Muir, Kafka's translator, Eliot's friend, and a worthy poet, remarked of Tolkien's trilogy: "The astonishing thing is that all the characters are boys masquerading as adult heroes."[4] The same might be said about Chesterton's characters: Adam Wayne, Patrick Dalroy, Evan MacIan, and Innocent Smith. In

---

3. Ibid., 179; Tolkien, *Return of the King,* 215.
4. Edmund Wilson and Edwin Muir, quoted in Pearce, *Tolkien,* 130.

Chesterton and Tolkien, sexuality is thoroughly eroticized, caught up in spiritual currents. Both authors reject Eliot's type of sex-consciousness. It can be suggested that the tradition will pardon their reticence, if modernism cannot. Compared to Tolkien, Chesterton shows a more deliberate artistry in infusing his heroes with boyish qualities of innocence and faith; the deliberate element is more palpable in Chesterton's case, because Chestertonian fiction is laced with satire. But Chesterton has a boyish streak even at his most serious: his soldiers and fighters are never far from the playing fields of their youth. It is part of Chesterton's idea of Englishness, his refusal of Kipling's cosmopolitanism. If Eliot had not been the international culture hero,[5] the Christian puerilities of *Four Quartets* might have excited more antipathy. There are not only the "the children in the apple-tree" to deal with, there is the Huck Finn of "The Dry Salvages" ("I do not know much about gods . . ."), with the Mississippi as Eliot's Derwent. It may seem odd to think of so imposingly mature a poem as showing any boyish feeling at all, but Eliot, likewise deliberate, includes the child in the man and gives a further meaning to the kingdom of heaven (Matt. 18:3). I offer these observations to underscore an aesthetic vice that is common to the modernist sensibility. I speak of the manner of the disillusioned child, for whom all wonder is a trap, for whom the goodness of the world must be entirely re-created, because the world has so badly failed to live up to expectations.

The question is whether the romance of history, as imagined by Chesterton, holds any promise after the horrors of the last century. For Eliot and Tolkien, the darkness is powerful but not final. For the anti-humanists, some of whom bear the stamp of Eliot's perceptions, the light has grown very dim indeed. Their answer is no. Like Goethe's Mephistopheles, they are the spirit that denies.

The words *romance* and *romanticism* must do considerable work if the question can even be asked. "For the very word 'romance,'" Chesterton writes, "has in it the mystery and the ancient meaning of Rome."[6] It is not just that, for Chesterton, the Roman origins of chivalry are evident. It is that the mystery and the meaning of Rome breathe life into history, making it more than the flux of matter. In the Eternal City

5. See Delmore Schwartz, "T. S. Eliot as the International Hero."
6. Chesterton, *Collected Works,* 1:212.

resides meaning: there we may find a providential narrative and the sacred rock upon which God has built his Church.

The mythic narrative is really a "double-plot," since the Roman world has always known a creative tension between Church and State. Matthew 22:21 ("Render . . . unto Caesar the things which are Caesar's; and unto God the things that are God's") was historically continuous with Roman religious policy. This longstanding "dual allegiance" has no parallel in Judaism or Islam.[7] The direct Jewish contribution to western civilization is, in this respect, the work of Romanized Jews. So long as one party (Church or State) does not crush the other, humanism can prosper. Literary authors can enter into exchanges with exegetes, theologians, rabbis, and saints. Arnold failed to grasp this crucial point—a failure that confirms his unfortunate relation to the diversity monolith. Making culture the servant of the State, he declared the State to be "sacred" and fell eloquently into the trap of Erastianism.[8] In a healthy culture, the line between religion and art, between the sacred and the profane, is never fixed: it is fluid and shifting. It is drawn and redrawn by the orthodox, as generations of writers make their impact known. There is no final line. For instance, it is loosely a fact that Dante's villain, Boniface VIII, springs from the same clericalist movement as Eliot's hero, Thomas à Becket, in reality a highly ambiguous figure. Dante drew creatively on the tension between Church and State, using his artistic genius to achieve a vision of justice, and seeing in the right relation of Church and State a central standard for politics and history. Eliot did much the same thing. Their historical judgments may clash, but Rome at least harbors the idea of a central standard. It furnishes history with an organic form: a complex, living structure of thought that is emphatically not the cornerstone of "fortress Catholicism."

Eliot and Tolkien lend considerable support to Chesterton's dream of Romanity.[9] Eliot, to cite a further example, renews an ancient perspective on Virgil: "His comprehensiveness, his peculiar kind of comprehensiveness, is due to the unique position in our history of the Roman Empire and the Latin language: a position which may be said

7. Eliot, *Idea of a Christian Society*, 44.

8. Arnold, *Complete Prose Works*, 5:223.

9. I adopt this useful term from Rémi Brague, *Eccentric Culture: A Theory of Western Civilization*.

to conform to its *destiny.*"[10] Like some monumental landscape of the imagination, the sublimity of this living tradition, which runs through Dante,[11] naturally tends to inspire receptivity and awe in thoughtful persons. Tolkien shows his devotion to Rome through Minas Tirith. He corrected the misperception that *The Lord of the Rings* was intended especially to sanctify northwest Europe: "The progress of the tale ends in what is far more like the re-establishment of an effective Holy Roman Empire with its seat in Rome than anything that would be devised by a 'Nordic.'"[12] Like Eliot, Tolkien wants to strike a balance between the center and the margin, a balance that is humanistic in its respect for culture.

I want to emphasize that the romance of history is not a triumphalist appeal to Rome or an unqualified plea for central authority. That would be absurd. Chesterton himself was fooled by the grandeur that was Mussolini (they met in 1929). Like Ezra Pound, Chesterton mistook Il Duce for a friend of Jeffersonian, "small-*r*" republicanism.[13] It is a failure that evokes the sad fatalism of *Gerontion,* and the blindness of every historian. Eliot observed the threat of classical rigidity in his *Coriolan* sequence, which ridicules the fascists:

> Here is the row of family portraits, dingy busts, all looking
>   remarkably Roman,
> Remarkably like each other, lit up successively by the flare
> Of a sweaty torchbearer, yawning.
> . . . .
> I a tired head among these heads
> Necks strong to bear them
> Noses strong to break the wind.[14]

The counterpoint to this flatulent, ceremonial boredom is a sensitive pastoral: "Come with the sweep of the little bat's wing, with the small flare of the firefly or lightning bug."[15] When Eliot completes the coun-

---

10. Eliot, *On Poetry and Poets,* 67–68.
11. See Highet, *Classical Tradition,* 73.
12. Tolkien, *Letters,* 376.
13. See Chesterton, *Collected Works,* 21:422.
14. Eliot, *Collected Poems,* 128.
15. Ibid.

terpoint by invoking the "Mantuan," he places the Virgil of *sunt lachri-mae rerum* before the Virgil of *imperium sine fine*. As Eliot suggests, Rome is open to many readings, classical and modern, irenic and imperial. But even within the broad arrangements of global Christianity, where it is imperative that each culture realize its way to Christianity without European strong-arming, the existence of a spiritual capital is needed for coordination and dialogue.

The romance of history is distinguished not by its coming to consciousness and power like manifest destiny, but by its uncanny pragmatism. It has a power that the will of itself cannot summarize; we cannot take credit for it, but we give credit to it. The working of this uncanny pragmatism is an indication of Providence and Truth; it operates in time in the realm of providential possibility, and its story is truer than Greek fatalism, bourgeois progressivism, or Marxist utopianism, the rival narratives of western man.[16] The Petrine text of the rock and keys in the Gospel of Matthew offers a good example: "And I tell you, you are Peter, and on this rock I will build my church, and the gates of Hades will not prevail against it. I will give you the keys of the kingdom of heaven, and whatever you bind on earth will be bound in heaven, and whatever you loose on earth will be loosed in heaven" (16:18–19 NRSV). At no point within the Gospel's historical setting were Peter's crucifixion and burial in Rome foreseeable. The possibility of late interpolation does not settle the matter. After the destruction of the temple in Jerusalem in AD 70, an act that dislocated the center of the early Church, weakening Jewish influence and indirectly strengthening Paul's mission to the Gentiles, the Church at Rome developed through natural processes of competition between rival groups. Its growth had a pragmatic element. It survived and prospered, based on its developing doctrines, on its growing resources, on the weird fact that Peter and Paul were martyred in Rome. As for the rock and keys, they found their way into the romance of Rome quite unexpectedly, quite uncannily, for to quote Paul Johnson: "There is no evidence that Rome exploited this text to assert its primacy before 250." Add to this that "there are no documented instances of anyone's ever being named 'rock'" in Greek (*Petros,* hence

16. I am indebted in my historical formulations to White, *Content of the Form,* 151.

Peter), and that the Aramaic *(Cepha)* was, at most, extremely rare if extant at all. Add, further, what Ronald Knox points out: "a comparison with Isaias xxii.22 will show the measure of the confidence" that Christ had in Peter.[17] But even leaving aside the strangeness of names and the prophetic role of Isaiah, two centuries is a long preparation, a long time for the rock and keys to orbit in the night of history.

The uncanny pragmatism of Rome takes many forms. There is the prophetic Virgil, planting seeds for the growth of Christianity on Roman soil. Like others in the Virgilian line, including Eliot and Tolkien, Chesterton can raise his voice after a long silence—and suddenly no novel written in the last century is more prescient than *The Flying Inn.* There is the miraculous survival of one of Rome's greatest historians, Livy, without whom the grand narrative of the West loses continuity and power. There is the emergence of Latin as western Europe's common language of learning, the mother tongue of modern science.

Most important for our concerns, there is the phenomenon of humanistic renewal known as a renaissance. Burckhardt saw a somewhat different spiritual dynamic from that of Christianity at work in the Italian Renaissance, but he quoted Dante's words with approval, "that the stones of the walls of Rome deserve reverence, and that the ground on which the city is built is more worthy than men say." Rather mysteriously or accidentally, while its worldly arm slept or exercised power elsewhere, Rome has kept its promise of rebirth many times. The Carolingian Renaissance is named for Charlemagne, who founded the Holy Roman Empire in a ceremony whose necessity was as strange to him as were its consequences. From the twelfth century onwards, there is the impact of Bernard of Clairvaux, whose "mysticism introduced a pathetic element into religion, which contained immense possibilities of growth." A gifted mystic and a superb writer, Saint Bernard was also a shrewd prelate up to his neck in worldly business. He built up the Cistercian Order, saw one of his pupils become pope, preached the Second Crusade (a failure), and renewed the foundations of European

---

17. Johnson, *History of Christianity,* 61; *The New Interpreter's Bible: A Commentary in Twelve Volumes,* 8:345–47; Ronald Knox, *The Belief of Catholics,* 125–26. Knox quotes the passage from Isaiah: "And I shall lay the key of the house of David upon his shoulder: and he shall open and none shall shut: and he shall shut and none shall open" (ibid., 126n4).

culture. And though he was a soul in search of the Word *(anima quaerens Verbum)*, his actions were finally incomprehensible to himself. A renaissance means a rebirth: one in which the uncanny pragmatism of books emerges. Rémi Brague reflects on the Greek classics, which survived because of Roman civilization: "what one might call the cultural bet of Europe is just that these ancient texts will always have something to teach us—and therefore, that they must be preserved in their literalness." For Brague, and I agree with him, the wager is not limited to the European continent. In our own time, when the death of Europe has entered the popular imagination, Pope Benedict XVI enlists the philosophical historian Alfred Toynbee to challenge the pyrrhic victory of European secularism. What Benedict finds in Toynbee is a voluntaristic vision, based on "the heritage of Christianity," and "focused on the energy of creative minorities and exceptional individuals."[18] In Benedict, the spirit of Christian humanism is active: his laudable intention is to avoid sectarian strife and to invigorate the great capacities for rebirth lying dormant in the western soul.

But for many scholars the term *renaissance* is outmoded. It is too metaphysical, too mythical, too European, for eyes fixed on "material culture," "print culture," and other sage delights. There is a terrible flatness in all this. The postmodern denial of grand narratives does not catch humanity in the round. It makes all heroism ironic. It trivializes the uncanny, spiritual pragmatism with which new authors recognize their teachers across distant ages, and renew the culture as they change it. It is even doubtful that "literalness" can be preserved by the specialists of "print culture," since they lack the means to distinguish reason from ideology. Language and literature demand conservation and historical consciousness: no one was more aware of this fact than Pater, a humanist after all. But ideologues exist to rationalize the necessity of change through all available means, including interpretation. Invariably they want to disrupt the natural and historical affinities that cohere within a national literature, and within the broadly European, western canon.

18. Jacob Burckhardt, *The Civilization of the Renaissance in Italy*, 108; Johan Huizinga, *The Waning of the Middle Ages: A Study of the Forms of Life, Thought, and Art in France and the Netherlands in the Dawn of the Renaissance*, 263; Brague, *Eccentric Culture*, 104; Arnold Toynbee, quoted in Joseph Ratzinger (Benedict XVI) and Marcello Pera, *Without Roots: The West, Relativism, Christianity, Islam*, 68; Ratzinger (Benedict XVI), *Without Roots*, 68; see also 120–24.

For Christian culture to survive, the *psychagogia,* or education of the soul, that Aristotle found in poetry must inform our Christian consciousness of history. We need to affirm a Christian poetics, an imaginative capacity for myth that is not hostile to reason and nature. We need to keep the tradition of humanistic scholarship alive, so that we may escape our current antirenaissance. And if we are fortunate, then Chesterton's defense of the world of man, like Aragorn's seemingly hopeless challenge at the Black Gate, will grow in our cultural memory. The history of Christianity is almost too daunting to think, but the stories of saints, heroes, and lovers, which come to life with each renaissance, may supply unexpected answers. There are hidden saints, unlikely heroes, and monsters breathing fire on the airwaves and the Internet. The patterns reveal themselves, shift and change and return, and they can die only in the ashes of our civilization. Such variations on the Roman mystery promise renewal and resurrection. We may sense their presence in life and in art. They haunt the coincidences and analogies of our historical experience, and they brush the mind with invisible wings.

It might be rejoined that we are all time's exiles. That is irrefutably the Christian condition. I suppose Christianity can survive the long haul in monasteries, in cloistered communities and islands in the storm. Middle-earth has a number of such sanctuaries, havens, and refuges. But Tolkien recognized the art of government in the Fourth Age, which was the Age of Man. The romance of Rome is not a story of otherworldly monasticism, but of engagement with the world. The rule of Saint Benedict laid the groundwork for European prosperity, literally by managing the land, and it enjoyed the papacy's support. The Benedictine model was never a total retreat. It grew as an alternative to the noble severity of Celtic monasticism. The Benedictines achieved a disciplined mean between this world and the next. They did not liberate the dynamism of Christianity, but they made the dynamism possible. Christopher Dawson, who rivals Chesterton in his insights into how culture incarnates religion, observes that Renaissance humanism was expressive of "Christian man, the human type that had been produced by ten centuries of ascetic discipline and intense cultivation of the inner life." It was this spiritual harvest that fostered "the new secular culture."[19]

19. Christopher Dawson, *Christianity and the New Age,* 96.

In the years ahead, amid the polarizing badness of social conflict, the Christian humanist must defend the radical middle, where genuine tolerance may be found. This means keeping orthodoxy in the public square. And this unfortunately means *Kulturkampf* or culture war, at least if the diversity regime insists on nothing less than marginalizing Christianity. The orthodox perspective is painful because it cuts deep into the defenses of the anti-Christian elite, by exposing their hypocrisy and intolerance. On the other hand, the Christian elite is also hypocritical and intolerant. Orthodoxy has the rhetorical and artistic means to create dialogue, but it will rightly be judged by its fruits. At its best, orthodoxy is inspired, mystical, pragmatic, and organic. It does not legislate to the world from an imperial height: rather, it emerges from inevitable social competition with heresy. To observe the persistence of powerful and ambitious heresies is to bear in mind what Montanists of every age are apt to forget, that orthodoxy requires sacrifice. As a creature of the radical middle, the Christian humanist follows Athanasius, "fighting," in Chesterton's words, "for that very balance of beautiful interdependence and intimacy, in the very Trinity of the Divine Nature, that draws our hearts to the Trinity of the Holy Family."[20] It may be true that every saint has a touch of the heretic, every heretic a touch of the saint. But it is orthodoxy (not heresy) that speaks to our most intimate moral awareness of each other and of God. Christian civilization is built on the deepest insights into our experience. Desiring more life, it keeps the fullest possible dynamic in play, and for all its tragic flaws confronts the destiny of humankind with hope.

Christianity and Islam are growing and competing. An estimated 12.4 percent of the world's population was Muslim in 1900. That number rose to about 20 percent in 2000. Western Christianity spoke for 27 percent of the world's population in 1900 and grew to roughly 30 percent a hundred years later.[21] This fact of competition cannot be ignored by the intellectually serious. Faith plays a role in how we live. Our ability to address its social impact reflects our integrity. If the well educated fail to discuss how religion shapes culture, if we cannot compare the Koran to the New Testament, if we tar Christian fundamentalists and al-Qaeda with the same brush, then we are constructing an

20. Chesterton, *Everlasting Man,* 233.
21. Samuel P. Huntington, *The Clash of Civilizations and the Remaking of the World Order,* 65.

alternative reality where religion is just a lifestyle choice and not the basis of people's lives. In the end, the construct will come crashing down around our ears. The humanistic way is to understand the relation between religion and modernity, and so to respect and encourage humanity.

Surprising to some, the decline of atheism likewise demands a critical response.[22] It compels us to acknowledge our species' deep innate need for religion, to get past the Marxist brainwashing, the shrill posturing and smug self-assertion that are the symptoms of withdrawal from reality. It indicates that of all the modern vanities, the vainest of all is free thinking that ignores the soul, for the soul is stronger than politics and will remake politics in its image. I do not say that atheism is necessarily wrong, but it may become irrelevant. The soul cannot be dismissed by rhetoric or biology, and scientific atheism defeats itself when it fails to honor traditional standards of humanistic tolerance. It is in our interest to recognize the true sources of tolerance in our culture, and certainly a genuine Christian humanism is scientific.

In 1909, in a book called *The Religious Attitude and Life of Islam,* Duncan Macdonald summarized the differences he saw between cultures: "*Inability,* then, to see life steadily, and see it whole, to understand that a theory of life must cover all the facts, and liability to be *stampeded* by a single idea and blinded to everything else—therein, I believe, is the difference between East and West."[23] Though it certainly isn't all that needs to be said on the subject, I suggest there is a hard nugget of truth in Macdonald's remark. There are, in my view, theological reasons why Christianity tends to achieve a greater degree of humanism than Islam tends to achieve. *Tends* is the word, for the differences are, from a humanistic perspective, not absolute. Under certain conditions, Islam, I necessarily and respectfully concede, can outperform Christianity in the field of culture.

Even so, I find myself staring at the angry ghost of Edward Said. In his famous book *Orientalism,* Said comments on the passage from Macdonald: "None of this, of course, is particularly new, from Schlegel to Renan, from Robertson Smith to T. E. Lawrence, these ideas get repeated and re-repeated. They represent a decision about the Orient,

22. Ibid.
23. Macdonald, quoted in Edward W. Said, *Orientalism,* 277.

not by any means a fact of nature."[24] It is not a triumph of pedantry to point out that Macdonald was in fact echoing Arnold's inaugural lecture as professor of poetry at Oxford:

> Now, the peculiar characteristic of the highest literature—the poetry—of the fifth century in Greece before the Christian era, is its *adequacy;* the peculiar characteristic of the poetry of Sophocles is its consummate, its unrivalled *adequacy;* that it represents the highly developed human nature of that age—human nature developed in a number of directions, politically, socially, religiously, morally developed—in its completest and most harmonious development of all these directions. . . . And therefore I have ventured to say of Sophocles, that he "saw life steadily, and saw it whole."[25]

Arnold is sensitive to historical differences, but he is confident in his humanistic approach. He works, as Said sardonically comments, from a tradition of "informed scholarship" and "rational inquiry." He is fairly capable of judging the strengths and weaknesses of different cultures, including his own. Some Englishmen, like A. N. Wilson, find him a snob: "for Arnold, almost everything he saw in his own country caused him to draw in his breath. The sheer vulgarity of modern England appalled him." Said takes the scapegoating further, burdening Arnold with xenophobia and racism: "For every idea about 'our' art spoken by Arnold . . . another link in the chain binding 'us' together was formed while another outsider was banished."[26] The choice of *banished* is striking, since banishment is ordinarily a deliberate act directed at an insider by other insiders. It is a word that reveals a fundamental confusion in Said's premises about social reality.

One intrinsic fact about traditions is that they are limited to the people who inherit them. A tradition is like a river: either you are born in its valley or you move into it or possibly you have never heard of it. Traditions are in this sense exclusive. They do not banish anyone, however. If you were not born in the Nile River valley, you are

24. Said, *Orientalism,* 277.

25. Arnold, *Complete Prose Works,* 1:28. He is quoting from his sonnet "To a Friend."

26. Said, *Orientalism,* 227; A. N. Wilson, *God's Funeral,* 260; Said, *Orientalism,* 228.

not banished from Egypt. The tradition of Arnold is continued and modified by Chesterton, Eliot, and Tolkien, who inherit shared premises about reason and nature, from which their significant differences emerge. We can safely say that Chesterton, Eliot, and Tolkien would have recognized Arnold's influence, and that Said chose to refer to Schlegel, Renan, Robertson Smith, and T. E. Lawrence. Samuel Huntington comes to Said's defense by pointing out that the "unity of the non-West and the East-West dichotomy are myths created by the West." But this statement, if it is to command the assent of truth and justice, cannot ignore the mythical aspect of all historical narratives, or the human need for generalization. Confronting the force of moral atomization in Ibsen and Shaw, Chesterton shot back: "what is the good of telling a man (or a philosopher) that he has every liberty except the liberty to make generalizations. Making generalizations is what makes him a man."[27] Individuals and traditions modify their generalizations over time for a variety of reasons. Macdonald's simple dichotomy of East and West may look simplistic, depending on the context of the discussion about East and West. As a plain matter of fact, the terms are used constantly today, and it is probably a good idea to try and say what we mean by them. For what is really at issue in Said's argument is our ability to generalize at all on the basis of western tradition. If we cannot, our tradition will obviously disintegrate. It already has in much of Britain, where a head teacher declared in 1995: "The common culture of pre-1940 England, based on the canon of English literature, the Whig interpretation of history and the liturgy of the Church of England, has died. . . . Life and language have outgrown the confines of English belief, history and ethnicity."[28] But so many deaths do not equal a birth. We can only hope that the British people do not follow their trailblazing pedagogues beyond "the confines of English belief," where they will reach the conclusion of a very bitter joke against themselves, having discovered without the utmost daring that it is easier to jump off a cliff than to climb one.

Marxism, like Islam, is a Christian heresy.[29] (Likewise, it can be said that Christianity is a Jewish heresy.) We find the spiritual inher-

---

27. Huntington, *Clash,* 33; Chesterton, *Collected Works,* 1:67.

28. Bernard Barker, quoted in Phillips, *Londonistan,* 63.

29. See, for example, Johnson, *History of Christianity,* 257; and White, *Content of the Form,* 142–43.

itance of Marxism to be more potent in Walter Benjamin, the most poetic member of the Frankfurt School, than in leading English Marxists like Raymond Williams and Terry Eagleton. This spiritual Marxism also enters into the work of American Marxist Fredric Jameson, long connected to Duke University. Jameson's historical bearings are quasi-theological. A "Marxist hermeneutic," he writes, "can be radically distinguished from . . . other types . . . , since its 'master code,' or transcendental signified, is precisely not given as a representation but rather as an *absent cause,* as that which can never know full representation."[30] A great deal hinges, in the end, on the degree to which the "absent cause" can be known through representation, not as something "given" or "full," but as historical knowledge that the hermeneut can wield with authority in the political realm.

Jameson rose to prominence in the 1980s with a highly theoretical essay called "Postmodernism, or The Cultural Logic of Late Capitalism." In it, he claimed to experience the look and feel of the future in LA's Bonaventure Hotel. Ironically, given our usual groveling at the altar of futurity, Chesterton had already hit on the essentials. In his "Meditation in a New York Hotel," from 1922, he described the "homelessness" of American social arrangements, the spectacular giganticism of modern machinery, and "the multitudinous modern repetitions" of manufacture and design in the new hotels. More, Chesterton studied "the plutocratic palace" for its the quasi-religious or cultic aspirations. He noticed the spiritual connotation of *elevator,* and he referred to "flying temples" much as Jameson refers to the "the glorious movement of the elevator gondolas." The key difference between the Christian and the Marxist is that the Marxist is more committed to mastering history and making predictions. Speaking for an "absent cause," Jameson is more judgmental about the state of people's minds, their world and their future, than Chesterton is, speaking for a present cause. And if we read Jameson's essay on "the cultural logic of late capitalism" for its predictive power, we must conclude that the author, in the essentials of his prophecy, has been falsified by the event. Tiananmen Square shook the world in 1989, the Berlin wall crumbled later the same year, the Soviet Union collapsed in 1991. There has been no "death of the bourgeois ego" and no "waning of affect" (Andy Warhol isn't the last word on art). The leading rock

30. Fredric Jameson, *The Ideologies of Theory: 1971–1986,* vol. 2, *The Syntax of History,* 149–50.

bands (for example, U2) are still the most tuneful and expressive; popular movies rely on the same old clichés and time-tested formulas. It appears that "'truth' itself" has not been entirely abandoned.[31]

Without the Gregorian calendar (AD 1582), which is based on the Julian calendar (46 BC) and starts with the birth of Christ according to the calculations of Dionysius Exiguus, who served Pope Gelasius I in the late fifth century, I fear we might be populating some twilight century where recorded dates mattered less to our lives than the collective will of the universities. For what is really shocking is Jameson's willfulness: I mean that to speak justly on behalf of the slaughtered and the brutalized we must be careful not to serve them up as ingredients of our historical self-consciousness, however dialectically purified we show ourselves to be; instead, restraint and love are called for, qualities nourished by Christianity and literature, not by ideology. The willfulness of even the best Marxist critics is a sign of Marxist cruelty. With a death toll of "between 85 million and 100 million" in the last century,[32] Marxism stands in plain sight like a giant axe-murderer, the blood dripping from his blade. Can the ideologue be expected to learn from this horror? It appears he will learn to slice his Marxism very fine. And the professor who fails to recognize that Marxism is a planetary killing machine is generally the same professor who dismisses Christianity as an anodyne for sheep.

Not that the Christian legacy is untouched by monumental evil. Paul Johnson has summed up the overall situation better than anyone:

> mankind without Christianity conjures up a dismal prospect. The record of mankind *with* Christianity is daunting enough. . . . The dynamism it has unleashed has brought massacre and torture, intolerance and destructive pride on a huge scale, for there is a cruel and pitiless nature in man which is sometimes impervious to Christian restraints and encouragements. But without these restraints, bereft of these encouragements, how much more horrific the history of these last 2,000 years must have been![33]

---

31. Chesterton, *Collected Works*, 21:51–61; Fredric Jameson, "Postmodernism, or The Cultural Logic of Late Capitalism," 83, 61, 63, 61.

32. Martin Malia, "Foreword: The Uses of Atrocity," x.

33. Johnson, *History of Christianity*, 517.

I fear this is honest to a fault: it tells the kind of hard truth that does not woo and flatter the young. It stands on a strict sense of reality, careful historical research, and mature powers of judgment. So the Christian humanist may be left defending what seems doubtful and dark, unless it is illuminated by learning.

Christianity resembles modern ideologies by combining mythology and metaphysics. This combination strengthens ideology's totalitarian hold, and it raises the specter of totalitarian Christianity. A Nazi judge told the leader of the 1944 plot against Hitler: "Count Moltke, Christianity and we Nazis have one thing in common and one only: we claim the whole man."[34] Actually, credal Nazism was grossly and conspicuously parasitic on Christianity, but the point to be gained is that Christianity offers means within itself for resisting totalitarian control, unlike Marxism, Nazism, or their busy progeny. It is dogmatically committed to real tolerance, and it holds immeasurable potential for truth, goodness, and beauty. By bringing its accumulated wisdom to the service of a democratic modernity based on real freedom, it can be the leading force for cultural renewal in the West. That is just its practical value. If I do not blush at the charge of being practical when I should be religious, it is because I cannot be practical at all without being religious.

34. Roland Freisler, quoted in Johnson, *History of Christianity*, 492.

Works Cited

Alexander, Neil M., ed. *The New Interpreter's Bible: A Commentary in Twelve Volumes.* 12 vols. Nashville: Abingdon Press, 1994–1998.

Aquinas, Thomas. *Essential Writings of Saint Thomas Aquinas.* Ed. Anton C. Pegis. New York: Random House, 1945.

Aristotle. *The Basic Works of Aristotle.* Ed. Richard McKeon. New York: Random House, 1941.

Arnold, Matthew. *The Poems of Matthew Arnold.* Ed. C. B. Tinker and H. F. Lowry. London: Oxford University Press, 1950.

———. *Poetry and Criticism of Matthew Arnold.* Ed. A. Dwight Culler. Boston: Houghton Mifflin, 1961.

———. *Complete Prose Works.* Ed. R. H. Super. 11 vols. Ann Arbor: University of Michigan Press, 1961–1977.

Ashbery, John. *Your Name Here.* New York: Farrar, Straus and Giroux, 2000.

Augustine. *The City of God.* Trans. Marcus Dods. New York: Modern Library, 1993.

———. *Confessions.* Trans. R. S. Pine-Coffin. London: Penguin Books, 1961.

Barzun, Jacques. *Classic, Romantic, and Modern.* Garden City, N.Y.: Doubleday, 1961.

———. *From Dawn to Decadence: 1500 Years of Western Cultural Life, 1500 to the Present.* New York: HarperCollins, 2000.

———. *A Stroll with William James.* Chicago: University of Chicago Press, 1983.

Bate, Walter Jackson. *The Burden of the Past and the English Poet.* Cambridge: Harvard University Press, 1970.

———. *Coleridge.* New York: Macmillan, 1968.

———. *From Classic to Romantic: Premises of Taste in Eighteenth-Century England.* 1946. Reprint, New York: Harper and Row, 1961.

Baudelaire, Charles. *The Painter of Modern Life and Other Essays.* Ed. and trans. Jonathan Mayne. London: Phaidon, 1965.

Beckett, Samuel. *The Complete Short Prose, 1929–1989.* Ed. S. E. Gontarski. New York: Grove Press, 1995.

———. *Mercier and Camier.* New York: Grove Press, 1975.

———. *Waiting for Godot: A Tragicomedy in Two Acts.* New York: Grove Press, 1956.

Beckett, Samuel, and Georges Duthuit. "Three Dialogues." In *Samuel Beckett: A Collection of Critical Essays,* ed. Martin Esslin, 16–22. Englewood Cliffs, N.J.: Prentice-Hall, 1965.

Birzer, Bradley J. *J. R. R. Tolkien's Sanctifying Myth: Understanding Middle-earth.* Wilmington, Del.: ISI Books, 2002.

Bishop, Elizabeth. *The Complete Poems, 1927–1979.* New York: Farrar, 1983.

Blake, William. *Blake's Poetry and Designs.* Ed. Mary Lynn Johnson and John E. Grant. New York: W. W. Norton, 1979.

Bloom, Harold. *Genius: A Mosaic of One Hundred Creative Minds.* New York: Warner Books, 2002.

———. Introduction to *T. S. Eliot: Modern Critical Views,* ed. Harold Bloom. New York: Chelsea House, 1985.

———. *Poetics of Influence: New and Selected Criticism.* Ed. John Hollander. New Haven, Conn.: Henry R. Schwab, 1988.

Bouyer, Louis. *Erasmus and His Times.* Trans. Francis X. Murphy. Westminster, Md.: Newman Press, 1959.

Bradley, F. H. *Ethical Studies.* 1876. 2d ed. Oxford: Clarendon Press, 1927.

Brague, Rémi. "Are Non-Theocratic Regimes Possible?" *Intercollegiate Review* 41 (spring 2006): 3–12.

———. *Eccentric Culture: A Theory of Western Civilization.* Trans. Samuel Lester. South Bend, Ind.: St. Augustine's Press, 2002.

———. *The Wisdom of the World: The Human Experience of the Universe in Western Thought.* Trans. Teresa Lavender Fagan. Chicago: University of Chicago Press, 2003.

Brooks, Cleanth. *Modern Poetry and the Tradition.* 1939. Reprint, New York: Oxford University Press, 1965.

Burckhardt, Jacob. *The Civilization of the Renaissance in Italy.* 1860. Trans. S. G. C. Middlemore. New York: Oxford University Press, 1945.

Bury, J. B. *The Idea of Progress.* New York: Macmillan, 1932.

Calder, John. *The Philosophy of Samuel Beckett.* London: Calder Publications, 2001.

Carey, John. *The Intellectuals and the Masses: Pride and Prejudice among the Literary Intelligensia, 1880–1939.* New York: St. Martin's, 1992.

Chaucer, Geoffrey. *The Riverside Chaucer.* Ed. Larry D. Benson. 3d ed. Boston: Houghton Mifflin, 1987.

Chekhov, Anton. *The Tales of Chekhov.* Trans. Constance Garnett. 13 vols. Hopewell, N.J.: Ecco Press, 1984.

Chesterton, G. K. *Collected Works.* General editors George J. Marlin, Richard P. Rabatin, and John L. Swan. 35 vols. San Francisco: Ignatius Press, 1986–.

———. *The Everlasting Man.* 1925. Reprint, Garden City, N.Y.: Image Books, 1955.

———. *The Flying Inn.* 1914. Reprint, Mineola, N.Y.: Dover, 2001.

———. "On Organization and Efficiency." 1921. In *Distributivist Perspectives.* Vol. 1, *Essays on the Economics of Justice and Charity,* ed. John Sharpe, 46–49. Norfolk, Va.: IHS Press, 2004.

———. *The Victorian Age in Literature.* New York: Henry Holt, 1913.

———. *What's Wrong with the World.* 1910. Reprint, San Francisco: Ignatius Press, 1994.

Childs, Donald J. *T. S. Eliot: Mystic, Son, and Lover.* New York: St. Martin's Press, 1997.

Coleridge, Samuel Taylor. *The Oxford Authors: Samuel Taylor Coleridge.* Ed. H. J. Jackson. Oxford: Oxford University Press, 1985.

———. *Shakespearean Criticism.* Ed. Thomas Middleton Raysor. 2 vols. London: J. M. Dent, 1960.

Collingwood, R. G. *The Idea of History.* 1946. Reprint, New York: Oxford University Press, 1956.

Cooke, Miriam. "Multiple Critique: Islamic Feminist Rhetorical Strategies." *Nepantla: Views from the South* 1, no. 1 (2000): 91–110.

Culler, A. Dwight, ed. *Poetry and Criticism of Matthew Arnold.* Boston: Houghton Mifflin, 1961.

Curtius, Ernst Robert. *European Literature and the Latin Middle Ages.* New York: Harper and Row, 1963.

Dawson, Christopher. *Christianity and the New Age.* London: Sheed and Ward, 1931.

D'Costa, Gavin. *Theology in the Public Square: Church, Academy, and Nation.* Oxford: Blackwell, 2005.

de Lubac, Henri, S.J. *The Drama of Atheist Humanism.* Trans. Edith M. Riley. Cleveland: Meridian Books, 1963.

Derrida, Jacques. "The Supplement of Copula: Philosophy *before* Linguistics." In *Textual Strategies: Perspectives in Post-Structuralist Criticism,* ed. Josué V. Harari, 82–120. Ithaca: Cornell University Press, 1979.

Dickstein, Morris. *Double Agent: The Critic and Society.* New York: Oxford University Press, 1992.

Dooley, David. Foreword to *Collected Works,* by G. K. Chesterton. General editors George J. Marlin, Richard P. Rabatin, and John L. Swan. 35 vols. 1:7–34. San Francisco: Ignatius Press, 1986–.

Downs, Donald Alexander. *Restoring Free Speech and Liberty on Campus.* New York: Cambridge University Press, 2005.

Eagleton, Terry. *Literary Theory: An Introduction.* Minneapolis: University of Minnesota Press, 1983.

Eliot, T. S. *After Strange Gods.* New York: Harcourt, 1934.

———. *Collected Poems, 1909–1962.* New York: Harcourt, 1988.

———. *The Complete Poems and Plays: 1909–1950.* San Diego: Harcourt, 1950.

———. *Essays Ancient and Modern.* New York: Harcourt, Brace, 1936.

———. *For Lancelot Andrewes: Essays on Style and Order.* Garden City: Doubleday, 1929.

———. *The Idea of a Christian Society.* 1939. Reprint, with *Notes towards the Definition of Culture,* in *Christianity and Culture.* San Diego: Harcourt, 1977.

———. *The Letters of T. S. Eliot, 1898–1922.* Ed. Valerie Eliot. San Diego: Harcourt, 1988.

———. "Notes on the Way." *Time and Tide* 16 (January 19, 1935): 88–90.

———. *Notes towards the Definition of Culture.* 1948. Reprint, with *The Idea of a Christian Society,* in *Christianity and Culture.* San Diego: Harcourt, 1977.

———. *On Poetry and Poets.* London: Faber, 1957.

———. *The Sacred Wood: Essays on Poetry and Criticism.* 1920. Reprint, London: Methuen, 1960.

———. *Selected Essays.* New ed. New York: Harcourt, 1950.

———. *The Selected Prose of T. S. Eliot.* Ed. Frank Kermode. New York: Harcourt, 1975.

———. *To Criticize the Critic and Other Writings.* 1965. Reprint, Lincoln: University of Nebraska Press, 1991.

———. *The Use of Poetry and the Use of Criticism.* 1933. Reprint, Cambridge: Harvard University Press, 1964.

Emerson, Ralph Waldo. *The Selected Writings of Ralph Waldo Emerson.* Ed. Brooks Atkinson. New York: Modern Library, 1968.

Empson, William. *Using Biography.* London: Chatto and Windus, 1984.

Ffinch, Michael. *G. K. Chesterton: A Biography.* London: Weidenfeld and Nicolson, 1986.

Flieger, Verlyn. "What Good Is Fantasy?" *Chesterton Review* 31 (fall–winter 2005): 217–21.

Freud, Sigmund. *Civilization and Its Discontents.* Ed. and trans. James Strachey. New York: W. W. Norton, 1961.

Fukuyama, Francis. *Our Posthuman Future: Consequences of the Biotechnology Revolution.* New York: Farrar, Straus and Giroux, 2002.

Gallup, Donald. *T. S. Eliot: A Bibliography.* London: Faber and Faber, 1969.

Gilson, Etienne. *The Christian Philosophy of St. Thomas Aquinas.* Trans. L. K. Shook, C. S. B. Notre Dame, Ind.: University of Notre Dame Press, 1994.

Goldstein, Warren. "What Would Plato Do? A (Semi-) Careerist Defense of the Liberal Arts." *Yale Alumni Magazine* 68 (July–August 2005): 36–43.

Grant, Robert M. *A Historical Introduction to the New Testament.* New York: Harper and Row, 1963.

Greenblatt, Stephen, ed. *The Norton Anthology of English Literature.* 8th ed. New York: W. W. Norton, 2006.

Guroian, Vigen. "On the Moral Imagination and Fairy Tales." *Chesterton Review* 31 (fall–winter 2005): 33–45.

Hamilton, Alice. "Samuel Beckett and the Gnostic Vision of the Created World." *Studies in Religion/Sciences Religieuses* 8 (summer 1979): 293–301.

Heidegger, Martin. *Basic Writings.* Rev. ed. Ed. David Furrell Krell. San Francisco: HarperSanFrancisco, 1993.

Herbermann, Charles G., Edward A. Pace, Condé B. Pallen, Thomas J. Shahan, and John J. Wynne, S.J., eds. *The Catholic Encyclopedia: An International Work of Reference on the Constitution, Doctrine, Discipline, and History of the Catholic Church.* 15 vols. New York: Robert Appleton, 1907.

Highet, Gilbert. *The Classical Tradition: Greek and Roman Influences on Western Literature.* 1949. New York: Oxford University Press, 1985.

Hill, Geoffrey. "T. S. Eliot Society Memorial Lecture." Paper presented at the annual meeting of the T. S. Eliot Society, Saint Louis, Mo., September 2002.

Houghton, Walter E. *The Victorian Frame of Mind.* 1957. Reprint, New Haven: Yale University Press, 1985.

Huizinga, Johan. *The Waning of the Middle Ages: A Study of the Forms of Life, Thought, and Art in France and the Netherlands in the Dawn of the Renaissance.* 1924. Trans. F. Hopman. Garden City, N.Y.: Doubleday Anchor, 1954.

Huntington, Samuel P. *The Clash of Civilizations and the Remaking of the World Order.* New York: Simon and Schuster, 1996.

Iannone, Carol. "Reading Literature: Decline and Fall." *Academic Questions* 18 (summer 2005): 6–15.

Jaeger, Werner. *Paideia: The Ideals of Greek Culture.* Trans. Gilbert Highet. 2d ed. New York: Oxford University Press, 1965.

James, William. *Writings, 1902–1910.* New York: Library of America, 1987.

Jameson, Fredric. *The Ideologies of Theory: 1971–1986.* Vol. 2, *The Syntax of History.* Minneapolis: University of Minnesota Press, 1988.

——— . "Postmodernism, or The Cultural Logic of Late Capitalism." *New Left Review* 146 (July–August 1984): 53–92.

Jay, Gregory S. *T. S. Eliot and the Poetics of Literary History.* Baton Rouge: Louisiana State University Press, 1983.

John Paul II. *Centesimus Annus.* 1991. http://www.vatican.va/holy _father/john_paul_ii/encyclicals/documents/hf_jpii_enc_01051 991_centesimus-annus_en.html

——— . *Fides et Ratio.* 1998. http://www.vatican.va/holy_father/john _paul_ii/encyclicals/documents/hf_jpii_enc_15101998_fides-et -ratio_en.html

————. *Memory and Identity: Conversations at the Dawn of the Millennium.* New York: Rizzoli International Publications, 2005.

Johnson, Paul. *Art: A New History.* New York: HarperCollins, 2003.

————. *Creators: From Chaucer and Dürer to Picasso and Disney.* New York: HarperCollins, 2006.

————. *A History of Christianity.* 1976. Reprint, New York: Simon and Schuster, 1995.

Johnson, Samuel. *Selected Essays from the Rambler, Adventurer, and Idler.* Ed. Walter Jackson Bate. New Haven: Yale University Press, 1968.

————. *Selected Poetry and Prose.* Ed. Frank Brady and W. K. Wimsatt. Berkeley and Los Angeles: University of California Press, 1977.

Jonas, Hans. *The Gnostic Religion: The Message of the Alien God and the Beginnings of Christianity.* 3d ed. Boston: Beacon Press, 2001.

Joyce, James. *The Critical Writings.* Ed. Ellsworth Mason and Richard Ellmann. New York: Viking Press, 1964.

————. *Dubliners.* New York: Viking Press, 1968.

Knox, Ronald. *The Belief of Catholics.* 1927. New edition, Garden City, N.Y.: Image Books, 1958.

Kors, Alan Charles, and Harvey A. Silvergate. *The Shadow University: The Betrayal of Liberty on America's Campuses.* New York: Free Press, 1998.

Kristeller, Paul Oskar. *Renaissance Thought: The Classic, Scholastic, and Humanist Strains.* New York: Harper and Row, 1961.

Larkin, Philip. *Required Writing: Miscellaneous Pieces, 1955–1982.* New York: Farrar Straus Giroux, 1982.

Lasch, Christopher. *The Revolt of the Elites and the Betrayal of Democracy.* New York: W. W. Norton, 1996.

Lewis, C. S. "Addison." In *Essays on the Eighteenth Century Presented to David Nichol Smith,* 1–14. Oxford: Oxford University Press, 1945.

————. *English Literature in the Sixteenth Century.* New York: Oxford University Press, 1954.

————. *Mere Christianity.* New York: Macmillan, 1960.

————. "Notes on the Way." *Time and Tide,* November 9, 1946, 1070–71.

Lewis, R. W. B. *Dante: A Penguin Life.* New York: Penguin, Lipper/Viking, 2001.

Lockerd, Benjamin, Jr. Untitled paper [in collection of the author].

Longman, Alastair H. B. *Gnostic Truth and Christian Heresy: A Study in the History of Gnosticism.* Peabody, Mass.: Hendrickson Publishers, 1996.

MacIntyre, Alasdair. *After Virtue.* 2d ed. Notre Dame, Ind.: University of Notre Dame Press, 1984.

Malia, Martin. "Foreword: The Uses of Atrocity." In *The Black Book of Communism: Crimes, Terror, Repression,* ed. Stéphane Courtois, Nicolas Werth, Jean-Louis Panné, Andrzej Paczkowski, Karel Bartoscaronek, Jean-Louis Margolin, ix–xx. Trans. Jonathan Murphy and Mark Kramer. Cambridge: Harvard University Press, 1999.

Maritain, Jacques. *Creative Intuition in Art and Poetry.* New York: Meridian Books, 1955.

———. *True Humanism.* Trans. Margot Adamson. New York: Charles Scribner's Sons, 1938.

Marsden, George M. *The Outrageous Idea of Christian Scholarship.* New York: Oxford University Press, 1997.

Menand, Louis. "An Introduction to Pragmatism." In *Pragmatism: A Reader,* ed. Louis Menand, xi–xxxiv. New York: Random House, 1997.

Mezciems, Jenny. "Swift's Praise of Gulliver: Some Renaissance Background to the *Travels.*" In *The Character of Swift's Satire: A Revised Focus,* ed. Claude Rawson, 245–81. Newark: University of Delaware Press, 1983.

Nagel, Thomas. *The Last Word.* New York: Oxford University Press, 1997.

Najarian, James. *Victorian Keats: Manliness, Sexuality, and Desire.* New York: Palgrave Macmillan, 2002.

Naylor, Thomas H. "Averting Self-Destruction: A Twenty-First-Century Appraisal of Distributivism." In *Distributivist Perspectives.* Vol. 1, *Essays on the Economics of Justice and Charity,* ed. John Sharpe, 17–26. Norfolk, Va.: IHS Press, 2004.

Nemoianu, Virgil. "Christian Humanism through the Centuries." *Image* 16 (summer 1997): 83–92.

Newman, John Henry. *The Idea of a University.* 1852. Reprint, ed. Frank M. Turner. New Haven: Yale University Press, 1996.

Nichols, Aidan, O.P. *The Shape of Catholic Theology: An Introduction to Its Sources, Principles, and History.* Collegeville, Minn.: Liturgical Press, 1991.

Nietzsche, Friedrich. *Basic Writings of Nietzsche.* Ed. and trans. Walter Kaufmann. New York: Modern Library, 1992.

————. *Thus Spoke Zarathustra: A Book for All and None.* 1883–1885. Trans. Walter Kaufmann. New York: Modern Library, 1995.

————. *Untimely Meditations.* Ed. Daniel Breazeale. Cambridge: Cambridge University Press, 1997.

Oser, Lee. "Coming to Terms with *Four Quartets.*" In *The Blackwell Companion to T. S. Eliot,* ed. David Chinitz. Oxford: Blackwell, forthcoming.

————. *The Ethics of Modernism: Moral Ideas in Yeats, Eliot, Joyce, Woolf, and Beckett.* Cambridge: Cambridge University Press, 2007.

Palevsky, Mary. *Atomic Fragments: A Daughter's Questions.* Berkeley and Los Angeles: University of California Press, 2000.

Pater, Walter. *Works.* Library ed. 10 vols. London: Macmillan, 1912–1915.

Pearce, Joseph. *Literary Converts: Spiritual Inspiration in an Age of Unbelief.* San Francisco: Ignatius Press, 1999.

————. *Tolkien: Man and Myth.* San Francisco: Ignatius Press, 1998.

————. *Wisdom and Innocence: A Life of G. K. Chesterton.* San Francisco: Ignatius Press, 1999.

Perl, Jeffrey. *Skepticism and Modern Enmity.* Baltimore: Johns Hopkins University Press, 1989.

Pétrement, Simone. *A Separate God.* Trans. C. Harrison. London: Darton, Longman, and Todd, 1991.

Phillips, Melanie. *Londonistan.* New York: Encounter Books, 2006.

Poirier, Richard. *Poetry and Pragmatism.* Cambridge: Harvard University Press, 1992.

Pound, Ezra. *Personae.* New York: New Directions, 1926.

————. Preface to *The Waste Land: A Facsimile and Transcript of the Original Drafts,* by T. S. Eliot. Ed. Valerie Eliot. New York: Harcourt, 1971.

Ratzinger, Joseph, and Marcello Pera. *Without Roots: The West, Relativism, Christianity, Islam.* Trans. Michael F. Moore. New York: Basic Books, 2006.

Ricks, Christopher. Introduction to *The Oxford Book of English Verse,* ed. Christopher Ricks. Oxford: Oxford University Press, 1999.

Rorty, Richard. "Postmodern Bourgeois Liberalism." *Journal of Philosophy* 80 (1983): 583–89.

Russell, Bertrand. *Mysticism and Logic*. 1917. Reprint, Totowa, N.J.: Barnes and Noble Books, 1981.

Said, Edward W. *Orientalism*. New York: Pantheon Books, 1978.

Saintsbury, George. *A History of English Literature: Elizabethan Literature*. New York: Macmillan, 1927.

————. *A Short History of English Literature*. New York: Macmillan, 1910.

Santayana, George. *Three Philosophical Poets: Lucretius Dante Goethe*. 1910. Reprint, Garden City, N.Y.: Doubleday [1938].

Schall, James V. *Schall on Chesterton: Timely Essays on Timeless Paradoxes*. Washington, D.C.: Catholic University of America Press, 2000.

Schopenhauer, Arthur. *The World as Will and Representation*. 1818. Reprint, trans. E. F. J. Payne. 3d ed. 2 vols. New York: Dover, 1966.

Schwartz, Delmore. "T. S. Eliot as the International Hero." *Partisan Review* 12, no. 2 (spring 1945): 199–206.

Shakespeare, William. *The Riverside Shakespeare*. Ed. G. Blakemore Evans. Boston: Houghton Mifflin, 1974.

Sharpe, John, ed. *Distributivist Perspectives*. Vol. 1, *Essays on the Economics of Justice and Charity*. Norfolk, Va.: IHS Press, 2004.

Sharrock, Roger. "Eliot's Tone." In *The Literary Criticism of T. S. Eliot*, ed. David Newton-De Molina, 160–83. London: Athlone Press, 1977.

Shelley, Percy Bysshe. *Shelley's Poetry and Prose*. Ed. Donald H. Reiman and Sharon B. Powers. New York: Norton, 1977.

Shippey, T. A. *The Road to Middle-earth*. Boston: Houghton Mifflin, 1983.

Shusterman, Richard. *T. S. Eliot and the Philosophy of Criticism*. New York: Columbia University Press, 1988.

Sokal, Alan, and Jean Bricmont. *Fashionable Nonsense: Postmodern Intellectuals' Abuse of Science*. New York: Picador, 1999.

Stratton, Arthur. *The Orders of Architecture*. 1931. Reprint, London: Studio Editions, 1986.

Swift, Jonathan. *Gulliver's Travels*. 1726. Ed. Albert J. Rivero. Reprint, New York: Norton, 2002.

Symons, Arthur. *The Symbolist Movement in Literature*. 1899. Reprint, New York: E. P. Dutton, 1958.

Taylor, Charles. *A Catholic Modernity?* Dayton, Ohio: University of Dayton, 1996.

————. *Sources of the Self: The Making of Modern Identity.* Cambridge: Harvard University Press, 1989.

Tolkien, J. R. R. *The Fellowship of the Ring.* 2d ed. Boston: Houghton Mifflin, 1993.

————. *The Hobbit.* 1937. 4th ed. Boston: Houghton Mifflin, 1978.

————. *The Letters of J. R. R. Tolkien.* Ed. Humphrey Carpenter. Boston: Houghton Mifflin, 1981.

————. *Poems and Stories.* Boston: Houghton Mifflin, 1994.

————. *The Return of the King.* 2d ed. Boston: Houghton Mifflin, 1993.

Tracy, David. *The Analogical Imagination: Christian Theology and the Culture of Pluralism.* New York: Crossroad, 1981.

————. *Dialogue with the Other: The Inter-Religious Dialogue.* Grand Rapids, Mich.: Wm. B. Eerdmans, 1991.

Ulmer, William A. *The Christian Wordsworth, 1798–1805.* Albany: State University of New York Press, 2001.

Vendler, Helen. *Part of Nature, Part of Us: Modern American Poets.* Cambridge: Harvard University Press, 1980.

————. Review of *The Varieties of Metaphysical Poetry,* by T. S. Eliot. *New Republic* 211 (December 19, 1994): 34–38.

————. *Soul Says: On Recent Poetry.* Cambridge: Harvard University Press, 1995.

Voegelin, Eric. *The New Science of Politics.* Chicago: University of Chicago Press, 1952.

Weigel, George. "Catholicism and Democracy." *Logos* 4, no. 3 (summer 2001): 36–64.

Wells, H. G. *The Outline of History: Being a Plain History of Life and Mankind.* Garden City, N.Y.: Garden City Publishing, 1930.

White, Hayden. *The Content of the Form: Narrative Discourse and Historical Representation.* Baltimore: Johns Hopkins University Press, 1987.

Whitehead, Alfred North. *Science and the Modern World.* 1925. Reprint, New York: Simon and Schuster, 1967.

Wilde, Oscar. *Complete Works of Oscar Wilde.* Ed. J. B. Foreman. New York: HarperCollins, 2001.

Williams, William Carlos. *Autobiography.* New York: New Directions, 1967.

Wills, Garry. *Chesterton: Man and Mask.* New York: Sheed and Ward, 1961.

Wilson, A. N. *God's Funeral.* New York: W. W. Norton, 1999.

Wordsworth, William. *Poetical Works.* Ed. Thomas Hutchinson and Ernest de Selincourt. Oxford: Oxford University Press, 1969.

Wright, N. T. *The Resurrection of the Son of God.* Minneapolis: Fortress Press, 2003.

Yeats, W. B. Introduction to *The Oxford Book of Modern Verse, 1892–1935,* ed. W. B. Yeats. New York: Oxford University Press, 1936.

Young, G. M. *Victorian England: Portrait of an Age.* 2d ed. 1953. Reprint, London: Oxford University Press, 1960.

INDEX

31, 123–24; values of, 27, 30, 50–
51, 129, 150; writing style of, 24,
35, 152. *See also* specific titles by
childishness, in characters, 151–52
Christ (Jesus), 65, 79
Christian apologists, 4, 24
Christian humanism, 133, 157;
history of, 12, 85; *Lord of the Rings*
as apology for, 65–66; role of, 159,
165
Christianity: attacks on, 11, 49, 83–
84, 91; characterizations of, 76,
127; Comte's humanism as
alternative to, 7; cults of
multiculturalism on, 85–86; culture
and, 5, 32, 33–35; global, 155;
history and, 151, 158; influence of,
113, 127–28; influences on, 12,
117; Islam's relation to, 29, 159–
61; in literature, 84, 97, 127–28;
marginalization of, 85, 91, 159;
myth in, 65–66, 84, 151; as
mythology, 65, 78; need for, 24, 84,
131, 148, 164; paradox in, 119,
128; role in history, 151, 155–57;
as story about truth *vs.* truth itself,
108; tragedy and comedy in, 127–
28; as unifying force, 30, 32–33;
values of, 60, 65, 83, 100n31, 127,
128–29, 164–65; Wordsworth's,
133. *See also* religion; Roman
Catholic Church
Church, 78, 133; Bernard of Clairvaux
building, 156–57; influences on,
16, 115; at Rome, 155; State and,
46–47, 50n40, 153. *See also*
Christianity; religion; Roman
Catholic Church
Church of England, Eliot joining, 40
City of God (Augustine), 113–14
civilization, 23, 126, 133, 157, 164;
competition of, 159–61; Jews'

contribution to, 153; outgrowing
Schopenhauer, 76–77. *See also*
culture
class, social, 22, 39, 122
classics, 44, 128, 157; Arnold on, 13–
14, 48; genres of, 138–39;
humanism and, 8, 129
Cocktail Party (Eliot), 89
Coleridge, Samuel Taylor, 6, 57, 94,
149; on fancy *vs.* imagination, 55–
56; Tolkien compared to, 56–58
Collingwood, R. G., 79
comedy, 127–28, 150
common sense, 22, 25
Comte, Auguste, 7, 14
Comtism, 6–7
Confessions (Augustine), 114
Conrad, Joseph, 25, 76
conscience, and nihilism, 62
Cosmic Will, 74–75, 78
Council of Nicaea, first, 6
creation, Schopenhauer on, 74–75
criticism, literary, 22, 99, 149;
philosophy of, 97–98, 130; poetry
as, 121, 124; self-revelation in, 92–
95
critics, 37; anti-Christian, 99–100;
Bloom as, 91–93, 99–100;
Shakespeare compared to, 100–101;
Vendler as, 86–90, 99–100
critics, literary: *vs.* critics at large:
Eliot on, 37
cult of suicide, 77
cults, of multiculturalism, 85
culture: in Chesterton's *The Flying Inn,*
33–35; Christian, 32, 158;
Christianity as beneficial to, 5, 165;
comparisons of, 48, 160–61, 161;
decline of, 11, 71–72, 107, 146–47;
European, 28–29; humanism and,
13, 48–49, 154; of Islam and
Christianity, 160–61; of Middle-

Pugin, A. W. N., 32, 148
Puritans, 13, 128

Rasselas (Johnson), 130–31
realism, 35, 112–13
reality, 74, 76, 106, 107, 147
reason, 62, 107–9, 140; Beckett and
  Schopenhauer using, 82–83;
  Chesterton on, 26, 34; faith and,
  22–23, 26, 34, 83; fantasy and, 59–
  60, 134; limitations of, 106, 110,
  113; need for realist base, 112–13;
  virginity of, 34–35. *See also* nature
  and reason
Red Book of Westmarch (Tolkien),
  66–67
"Reflection on 'Vers Libre'" (Eliot),
  137–38
Reformation, effects of, 115
religion, 65, 115, 156, 160; arts and,
  148, 153; as bulwark against
  tyranny in democracy, 46, 49;
  competition between, 159–61;
  crisis of, 41; culture and, 12, 33–
  35, 158; eastern, 74; education and,
  44–45, 49–50; importance of, 22,
  50, 160; pragmatism freeloading
  on, 98–99; Roman, 153; science *vs.*,
  8, 14; sophisticates' distaste for, 87–
  88; tolerance in, 5. *See also*
  Christianity; Church
Religion of Humanity, 8
Religious Attitude and Life of Islam
  (Macdonald), 160–61
renaissance, 156–57
Renaissance humanism, 8–9, 12, 158
Renaissance (Pater), 95
"Rethinking William James" (Tracy),
  110–11
revolution, Tolkien hoping for, 62
Richards, I. A., 17
"Robot Age," 62

Roman Catholic Church, 7, 112;
  Chesterton and, 32, 51; liberal, 15–
  16; modernism and, 99, 105;
  romanticism and, 57–58. *See also*
  Christianity; Church; religion
romance, 75, 150; breaking of vows
  and, 146–47; Chesterton on, 152–
  54; of history, 152, 155; of Rome,
  155, 158
romanticism, 94, 133, 135, 151;
  Eliot's, 129–30; Tolkien's, 56–58
Rome: Augustine on, 113–14;
  pragmatism of, 155–56; romance
  and, 152–55, 158
Rorty, Richard, 97–99
Ruskin, John, 32, 148
Russell, Bertrand, 26
Russia, 16

Sacred Wood (Eliot), 37, 40, 94, 135
Sade, Marquis de, 80n18
Said, Edward, 160–62
Saintsbury, George, 136–37, 139–40,
  149
Saint-Simon, 7
Saint Thomas Aquinas: The Dumb Ox
  (Chesterton), 50
salvation: literature and, 128, 131; in
  Waiting for Godot, 81–82
Santayana, George, 123
Sauron (in *Lord of the Rings*), 63
Schall, James, 146
Schopenhauer, Arthur, 74–78, 81–82
science, 113, 125; Arnold and, 12–14;
  humanism and, 8, 13; humanizing
  perspective on, 126–27; impact of,
  39–40; laws of, 7, 23; limitations
  of, 11, 60–62; poetry and, 8, 126,
  133; reception of, 125–26; religion
  and, 8, 14; theology and, 11, 112;
  truth and, 21–22, 60–61
Second Vatican Council, 105